MARVEL
AGE OF
COMICS

DAREDEVIL: BORN AGAIN

AN EXPLORATION BY

CHRIS RYALL

BLOOMSBURY ACADEMIC
NEW YORK • LONDON • OXFORD • NEW DELHI • SYDNEY

BLOOMSBURY ACADEMIC
Bloomsbury Publishing Inc, 1359 Broadway, New York, NY 10018, USA
Bloomsbury Publishing Plc, 50 Bedford Square, London, WC1B 3DP, UK
Bloomsbury Publishing Ireland, 29 Earlsfort Terrace, Dublin 2, D02 AY28, Ireland

BLOOMSBURY, BLOOMSBURY ACADEMIC and the Diana logo are
trademarks of Bloomsbury Publishing Plc

MARVEL PUBLISHING
Jeff Youngquist, VP, Production and Special Projects
Brian Overton, Manager, Special Projects
Sarah Singer, Editor, Special Projects
Jeremy West, Manager, Licensed Publishing
Sven Larsen, VP, Licensed Publishing
David Gabriel, VP, Print & Digital Publishing
C.B. Cebulski, Editor in Chief

BLOOMSBURY ACADEMIC
Haaris Naqvi, Global Editorial Director
Leah Babb-Rosenfeld, Editorial Director
Hali Han, Assistant Editor
Ian Buck, Deputy Head of Production
Zeba Talkhani, Senior Production Editor
Ben Anslow, Senior Designer

First published in the United States of America 2025
Reprinted 2025

© 2025 MARVEL

Cover art: David Mazzucchelli
Cover design: Ben Anslow
Original story: Frank Miller

Bloomsbury Publishing Inc does not have any control over, or responsibility for, any third-party
websites referred to or in this book. All internet addresses given in this book were correct at
the time of going to press. The author and publisher regret any inconvenience caused if
addresses have changed or sites have ceased to exist, but can accept no responsibility for any
such changes.

Library of Congress Control Number: 2025018545

ISBN: PB: 979-8-7651-3168-8
          ePDF: 979-8-7651-3170-1
          eBook: 979-8-7651-3169-5

Series: Marvel Age of Comics

Typeset by RefineCatch Limited, www.refinecatch.com
Printed and bound in India

For product safety related questions contact productsafety@bloomsbury.com.

To find out more visit www.bloomsbury.com/marvel-books

"I intend to have a bookshelf of my work that lives forever"
– Frank Miller

CONTENTS

ORIGINAL CREDITS

Daredevil (1964) #227–233

Frank Miller
WRITER

David Mazzucchelli
ARTIST

Christie Scheele (#227, #229–233) and Richmond Lewis (#228)
COLOR ARTISTS

Joe Rosen
LETTERER

Ralph Macchio
EDITOR

Jim Shooter
EDITOR IN CHIEF

Introduction: *Born* Under a Bad Sign

The story begins not in Hell's Kitchen, Daredevil's New York hang, but rather in a dingy Mexican motel room: the unmaking of a hero. The laying bare of a masked adventurer's deepest secrets. That's where the revelation of Daredevil's closely guarded secret identity—that of blind lawyer Matt Murdock—starts him and his loved ones on a path more treacherous than any threat he has faced before.

This is where *Daredevil #227,* the first chapter in the seven-part saga that's come to be known as "Born Again," begins. *Daredevil #227* is also where writer Frank Miller, who previously wrote and drew Daredevil's exploits to great acclaim, made his full-time return to the series. He did so as writer only this time around, joining the series' regular artist, David Mazzucchelli, on a character-defining storyline that has had lasting resonance. This work is considered one of the high points of 1986, considered by many to be perhaps the best year for super hero comics stories. It's perhaps only matched in stature by another industry high from 1986 also created by Miller and Mazzucchelli, that one featuring the early days of a certain pointy-eared dark knight detective. "Born Again" launched a few months prior to their other series, "Batman: Year One," and so provided the first look at what a special pairing this would be.

It certainly was that for me, a teenager who even at that point in my life had been reading comics for a decade and felt ready for comics to age along with me.

1986 delivered that in so many ways—many of them due to Frank Miller.

My first awareness of Frank's art came a few years prior. A cover here, a pin-up there. But it wasn't until my local comic retailer put a copy of *Daredevil* #181 in my hand and said "here, kid, you'll like this one" that I truly got a sense of what Frank Miller had to say as a creator. As per usual, my retailer knew just what I'd like. That issue, coming as it did a year into Frank's first stint as writer and artist, with the added benefit of being inked and often colored by Klaus Janson, felt custom-tailored to my tastes. Though the earlier issues of their run were pricey for a non-working pre-teen, I found ways—chores, a paper route, begging (the former two far more effective than the latter)—to track down the rest of their work.

It was something special to me then, and remains so now. When Miller departed the series, it felt like comics would never be that good again. (Keep in mind, I wasn't even able to drive yet when I had this thought. I had decades of comic-reading years still ahead of me.) No matter who took over the series next, it couldn't possibly compare.

I stuck with it. Frank had managed to make me care wholly about a title I never bothered with before.

It wasn't the same but it was okay by me. Still, the enthusiasm with which I greeted the announcement of Frank's impending return, especially alongside current series artist David Mazzucchelli, who'd been so impressive of late, was palpable.

Still, as I've come to discover over the years, announcements of a second bite at the nostalgia apple most often don't—can't—live up to expectations. Current circumstances, continued life experiences, and the evolution of the kinds of stories creators might be interested in telling at that point rarely align in ways that deliver that same visceral thrill as a first experience.

So imagine my surprise, my utter joy, when the work Miller and Mazzucchelli created together exceeded all of my high expectations. "Born Again" and its furtherance of Matt Murdock's story without relying on so many of the fan-favorite elements that made Miller's first go-round so well-loved was pure rocket fuel for me. The months between issues were interminable. Each issue's release was an experience to be savored. And what the two creators delivered has remained one of the most lasting, resonant, and flat-out best super hero comic experiences I've ever had. The dialogue flows for me like song lyrics. The art and colors are so vivid and gorgeous even without all the modern enhancements that so many comics have adopted over the intervening years.

Not that I necessarily need to sing its praises the way I have over the years since "Born Again" remains beloved by so many, but I've never passed up a chance to recommend the story to anyone who will listen. And the fact that you've picked up this first volume in Bloomsbury's line of Marvel Age of Comics explorations indicates that you're either interested in what makes "Born Again" so special, or you're already aware of it and want to revisit it in all the ways I explore its greatness here, or perhaps both. Either way, I hope this book accomplishes its goal, which is to make you want to read "Born Again" again and be reminded of what a special series, what a great creative pairing, and what a unique time in comics it was.

It's hard to express now just how much Miller's return to writing *Daredevil* raised the stakes for characters in then-unheard-of ways. Add to that the fact that artist David

Mazzucchelli was on a rapid artistic rise at the time he and Miller joined forces, and the pieces were in place for their first partnership to be something truly special.

Ralph Macchio, the editor responsible for Miller's return to the title, had been impressed by Miller's earlier time writing the series, and felt that *Daredevil* in the right hands had the potential to be Marvel's equivalent of DC's *Batman*, a perennial best-seller. Macchio and I spoke at length on the cusp of "Born Again's" fortieth anniversary about how this storyline first came together. Macchio stated that he saw the idea of bringing Frank back to *Daredevil* as "a great opportunity. Frank had the history and the understanding of the character to make it work all over again."

Once Miller was on board to return, what the team didn't do was run around telling everyone that Frank Miller was back on the book. As Macchio told me, "We just quietly put the book together, and then suddenly, word got out that Frank Miller was back on *Daredevil*. And from there, it just took off. They did a spectacular job. I mean, if you've never read a *Daredevil* story, you could just read 'Born Again' and you'd know everything you need to know about Matt Murdock, Daredevil, and his world."

But even with the high level of anticipation over the return of the fan-favorite Miller, the seven issues that comprise "Born Again" shocked and delighted legions of readers then and now. The genius of Miller and Mazzucchelli's "Born Again" is that it not only built well on Miller's earlier interpretation of the character and his place in a darker corner of the Marvel Universe, it did so without abandoning all parts of the series' previous two years' worth of stories written by comic legend Dennis O'Neil and drawn in large part by Mazzucchelli.

Yet the sum was still something greater than its composite parts.

For one thing, as resonant as Miller's artistic interpretation of Daredevil was in his first go-round on the series, Miller's ability to now focus on writing full scripts and leave the artistic presentation to another artist helped him focus on a new level of nuance and emotional resonance that transcended his earlier run. If Miller's previous time as *Daredevil*'s writer/artist provided him with a deep understanding of the core of the character—what it was about Matt Murdock/Daredevil that made him unique in the Marvel Universe—"Born Again" served as the storyline that allowed Miller to upend the character, destroying Matt Murdock's personal and professional lives, his reputation, and his support system. In "Born Again," Daredevil loses his identity, his job, and, for a time, his sanity, leaving him a character devoid of reason or hope, at least until he rediscovers the essence of who he is underneath it all.

Likewise, artist David Mazzucchelli was, at the time of "Born Again," still a relative newcomer to comics. He'd been the primary artist on *Daredevil* for the two years prior to Miller's return, and his earlier issues displayed flashes of brilliance that felt fully realized by the time he began working on "Born Again." Mazzucchelli's style echoed in some ways that of former *Daredevil* artist Gene Colan—both had a tendency to use detailed naturalism and ample shadows in their work to create moody settings for the characters to inhabit. Once Mazzucchelli began inking his own pencils prior to Miller's return, these specific enhancements came through even more. Over a relatively short span of time, Mazzucchelli found his artistic voice, then, in "Born Again," leveled up in ways that transcended even his earlier highs, before ultimately growing stylistically past the point of desiring to tell super hero stories any longer.

Ahh, but for a time, *Daredevil* had them both: Miller and Mazzucchelli, along with colorist Christie Scheele, who provided a stunning level of depth and suffuse lighting to "Born Again" that was unlike many super hero comics of its time.

As "Born Again" opens in a dusty Mexican motel room, Daredevil's former girlfriend Karen Page sits, her sweaty clothes clinging to her undernourished frame. Pale yellow sunlight filters in through mini-blinds, casting the room in equal parts pale light and dark shadow.

Karen had left New York and Matt Murdock years before to seek fame and fortune as a Hollywood actress. She was always a sunny character, and so her leaving New York for an even sunnier climate made perfect sense. Karen Page, blonde, beautiful, and as positive and cheerful a character as any Marvel character from the 1960s, walked out of Matt's life and, readers assumed, into a different kind of fame and fortune.

As readers, we assumed that all had gone according to her plan.

Until we witnessed her in the opening scene of #227, sitting slumped in a chair, her body language laying bare her present-day defeat, her pathetic need. This is a new Karen Page, one run ragged by addiction; a Karen Page desperate enough to try to temporarily quell her withdrawal anguish by selling the one remaining item of value in her life—Matt Murdock's secret identity.

As a regular reader of the series, and one of many who was greatly anticipating Miller's return, as enamored with his previous time on the title as I was, I was still floored by the quiet power of this opening scene. If Karen Page, sunlight personified, was in such a desperate state as *this* on chapter one page one, what was possibly going to happen from here?

Nothing expected. And certainly nothing good.

What played out over those seven issues was so much more gripping than what readers like me could have imagined taking place in a monthly Marvel comic. So much more lasting, far beyond the year in which these stories took place. To today and beyond, in fact.

Miller and Mazzucchelli went about presenting the destruction of a beloved Marvel hero in as methodical a way as any plan ever executed by a comic-book super villain. In this series' case, that villain would be the Kingpin of Crime, whose quest to tear down a good man had unforeseen and lasting impact for them both.

In the process of stripping bare all we thought we knew about Matt Murdock's costumed alter ego, Miller and Mazzucchelli then rebuilt the character slowly, agonizingly, and realistically, helping put Matt Murdock back on a path to rediscover what was truly important in his life. The essence of what it means to be a hero. How to rise from an impossibly bleak place to being truly born again.

There have been other comic-book series where a hero's secret identity was revealed to loved ones and arch-enemies alike. In fact, that's been one of the most-often-visited storylines in comics dating back to the earliest days of stories about masked adventurers. But there has never been a story involving that trope quite like this one.

It began in a motel room in Mexico. Where the story goes after that, and the disparate ways that "Born Again" captivated readers, changed both the character and the very conversation around secret identities. The many ways in which it influenced future comics creators is what this volume is going to reveal.

In the case of this volume, focusing on *Daredevil: Born Again*, that means a deep dive into not only the dazzling story and gorgeous art on display throughout its seven chapters, but also look at the events leading up to "Born Again," the characters' interpersonal relationships and the creators' impact on those developments, the ways "Born Again" dug deep into the concept of identity and heroics, the broader impact of a character's choice to fight crime as a masked hero while trying to keep friends and loved ones separate from such a lifestyle choice, and as pertains to Matt Murdock's specific decline in the first half of "Born Again," a discussion of the various aspects of mental illness on vivid display in this storyline, too.

There's another component of "Born Again" on display in the comics and discussed at length here, too. The titular hero suffers both a mental and physical breakdown the likes of which was rarely if ever seen in a Comics Code Authority-approved super hero title before. And the way the creators handle Matt Murdock's mental health crisis deserved further exploration, in terms of how it was handled and the various disorders on display. This is certainly more of a discussion today than it was in super hero comics from nearly four decades past, but that makes the portrayals in this series all the more notable for their accuracy and sensitivity.

Miller's work on the series was influential to both creators who followed him on the series and beyond. I discuss the story's impact on future series writers as well as Daredevil's portrayal in other media, and the ways Frank Miller's work has influenced those interpretations, too.

By the end, if I've done my job right, you'll not only want to go back and revisit this one for yourself but also have a greater understanding of the many reasons why the work these creators produced nearly forty years ago still matters in so many different ways.

Welcome to *Marvel Age of Comics: Daredevil: Born Again.* Check your conceptions about the character and its creators at the dingy motel-room door.

1

Fallen *Devil*

As *Daredevil: Born Again* opens, Matt Murdock/Daredevil is a character on the edge. He's reeling from recent losses, he has grown suspicious of his alliances after a splintering of his law practice and friendship with his partner and oldest friend, Foggy Nelson, and he's even more prone to bursts of anger and violence than he already was. Murdock's patience and occasional stoicism, in the face of extreme odds, are no more; and all of these shifts in his mood are exacerbated by feelings of deeply embedded Catholic guilt that he feels about his part in all of this. His nerves are frayed, his hold on his sanity even more precarious than it has been in his often-troubled past.

In short, this is not the usual circumstances in which readers often find costumed heroes at the start of a story, but this sort of fractious state of affairs isn't exactly a new place for Matt Murdock to find himself.

*

When Frank Miller first took over the regular penciling duties on *Daredevil* in the late 1970s, the character's transition from being a wise-cracking costumed adventurer in the Spider-Man mold was already well under way.

Which was quite an evolution from where the character began in his 1964 debut. When first introduced to readers, the character was very much in the vein of Spider-Man, a devil-may-care hero clad in two-tone tights.

Daredevil #1's cover was drawn by Jack Kirby and series artist/co-creator Bill Everett. Daredevil is shown smiling and leaping in a red-and-yellow circus-strongman-like costume. If his pose looks reminiscent of Spider-Man, that's intentional—the cover not only includes an inset image of Spidey but also includes as a description stating that Daredevil is carrying on in the tradition Spider-Man started.

The cover also showcases the three series leads, described in cover copy as "the Most Unusual Hero of all, Matt Murdock, fun-loving Foggy Nelson [and] gorgeous Karen Page." As they first appeared, all three were pretty fun characters. Like Spider-Man, Daredevil mostly wise-cracked his way through fights against somewhat goofy villains. The character's blindness was really the only trait that made him unique at the time.

In the latter half of the dour 1970s, *Daredevil* writer Roger McKenzie took the character down a darker path, downplaying his earlier, more fanciful costumed villains like the buffoonish Jester and comical Stilt Man, in favor of street-level criminals, assassins, and assorted gangsters and death-dealers.

At that time, inker Klaus Janson contributed added grit through his heavy use of shadows, surrounding the reader with darkness not seen since the early days of the title when it was drawn with cinematic flair by Gene Colan. Klaus Janson was a good fit for any of the pencilers who worked on the series, artists like Gil Kane or Bob Brown, but he finally found a true artistic kindred spirit in Frank Miller.

When the then-neophyte artist Miller became the regular penciler as of *Daredevil* #158, the art team felt even more well-attuned to the stories McKenzie was telling. Together, this trio moved *Daredevil* deeper into the shadowy corners of the Marvel Universe's New York. While Spider-Man swung on web lines high above the New York city streets, Daredevil's world was one now filled with dark and dangerous alleyways, deserted waterfront warehouses, and shadowy rooftops.

A year after taking over as series artist, Miller also started writing the series, too. The Miller/Janson era kicked off with a bang in issue #168, their first issue as the series' creative team. In that issue, Miller introduced a character who became an immediate fan-favorite, Matt Murdock's former college-girlfriend-turned-ninja-assassin, Elektra. Fans at the time assumed her appearance was a one-off, but when she returned the next issue and became one of the key focal points over the next year's stories, the book exploded in popularity. This deluge of new readers led to the title's change in frequency, as it moved from a bi-monthly book to one of Marvel's best-selling titles month after month.

Miller wasn't through shaking up the title, either. Just one year after introducing Elektra, Miller killed her off (well, the assassin Bullseye killed her, and with her own weapon, too) in the extra-length "One Lives, One Dies!" issue, #181. Her death then set in motion events that continued on long past Miller's time as the series' writer/artist, which concluded with *Daredevil* #191. Matt Murdock was changed by Elektra's death. First, he remained in denial that she was truly done, which echoed the sentiment of many of the angry letter-writing fans. And then, after going so far as to exhume her body to verify her death, he became embroiled in a storyline involving ninja mystics that resulted in Elektra's reincarnation (a detail unbeknownst to Matt Murdock). Miller did exit the title one issue later, but he continued to use Elektra in two miniseries set in the past and one graphic novel that brought her back into Matt Murdock's life, only to kill her one final time. But this being serialized comics, after all, the character would eventually resurface, eventually even assuming the costume and moniker of "Daredevil" herself.

Along the way, the character of Matt Murdock changed,

becoming more grim, less trusting. There was general darkening of the stories told in comics in the early-to-mid-1980s, and Miller's work has long been cited as one of the key facilitators of this. Moreso for "Born Again" and a couple other miniseries from that same year, but it was evident even here in his initial run.

But even amidst all of this darkness and death, and the resultant guilt Matt Murdock now carried around after Elektra's death, Miller stated after he left the title that he never regarded Daredevil the character as an overly grim avenger. As Miller was quoted as saying in trade magazine *Amazing Heroes* #69 (April 1985), "He's a much warmer character than [DC's Batman]. He's much more personally involved. Daredevil is interacting with his environment, but he is that same kind of savage, primal thing."

It was in Miller's first run on *Daredevil* that he also reinvigorated a character who had largely been considered one of the jocular Spider-Man's primary villains: the larger-than-life mobster Wilson Fisk, also known as the Kingpin. After the conclusion of Miller's first run on the title, Daredevil and the Kingpin would be inexorably linked, the two characters serving as perfect foils for one another, with each occasionally seeing the usefulness of the other. Until "Born Again," that is.

It's with this status quo that subsequent writer (and former series editor) Dennis O'Neil found himself after picking up the scripting reigns from Miller. Matt Murdock, on edge and reeling from Elektra's death, meets Irish photographer Glorianna O'Breen, a potential new love interest. But as with so many of his relationships, Murdock's time with Glorianna is complicated by the time he spends risking his life as a costumed adventurer, as well as by his repeated refusal to take time to properly mourn Elektra. Not long after, Murdock also has to contend with another tragic loss, that of his former fiancée Heather Glenn. In the pre-Miller era of *Daredevil*, Glenn was the daughter of a rich and corrupt industrialist who, upon her father's death (a circumstance for which she blamed Matt Murdock, for a time), Heather assumed control of his company. But even then Murdock never took her travails seriously enough, so caught up was he in his own drama. Which ultimately resulted in Glenn taking her own life.

All of which also took its toll on Murdock's working partnership with longtime friend Foggy Nelson. Murdock began to withdraw from those around him, bearing all of his burdens on his own as best he could.

Nearing the conclusion of O'Neil's time on the title, Frank Miller returned to script one other issue prior to "Born Again": a standalone story presented in *Daredevil* #219. In that issue, titled "Badlands," a plain-clothed Matt Murdock wanders into an industrial town called Broken Cross, a rundown area "curled up like a wino off the New Jersey Turnpike." This setting is provided with additional grit by the art team of penciler John Buscema and inker Gerry Talaoc, who bring rough-hewn lines to the broken-down town and its equally shattered residents.

In that issue, Matt Murdock, clad in jeans, a dark jacket, hat, and sunglasses, never utters a word. He is both stoic and grim as he is pulled deeper into the damaged town's collective trauma. Something about his inherent goodness stands out to the few residents who do their best to resist the town's corruption. Years prior, an uncorrupt cop named John Fagan likewise resisted the dark forces in town and was murdered as a result. The town lost all hope in his absence, at least until Murdock came to town. Something in the way Murdock resists the bad cops and violent lowlifes he runs into inspires the townspeople to fight back. They do so, albeit with tragic consequences. Still, when all is said and done, the town seems headed for a brighter future. Murdock, who recedes into the shadows of the night, does not.

Even with Miller's momentary return on that issue, fans at the time had no idea that a longer stint was looming. In the pre-internet era of the mid-1980s, the first real inkling fans had about Miller's looming return alongside artist David Mazzucchelli came on the pages of *Marvel Age Magazine* #36, released in 1986 only a few issues before Miller's first "Born Again" issue.

Marvel Age was a monthly promotional magazine released by the company to tease details about upcoming releases, feature interviews with writers and artists, and generally hype upcoming series and storylines to a fan base that was otherwise devoid of such official expansive details.

The issue, which featured a striking cover image of Daredevil and bold copy reading, simply, "MILLER AND MAZZUCCHELLI ON DAREDEVIL," had an extended article about Frank Miller's return to the character's monthly title, as well as on two separate Daredevil-related graphic novels.

The article detailing Frank's plans for the monthly series was purposely vague, stating only that "Daredevil's first girlfriend, Karen Page, will be back, but not the way you'd expect! Foggy Nelson and Glorianna O'Breen will be playing increasingly large and surprising roles! And Daredevil will be betrayed by one of his closest and most trusted friends!"

Miller returned one issue prior, in a hand-off story co-written with O'Neil. That comic, *Daredevil* #226, delved deeper into the ever-more-fractured state of Murdock's psyche that O'Neil had been exploring in his run. The issue set all the pieces in place for the fall and rise to come in "Born Again."

This aligned with Miller's stated plans in *Marvel Age* #36. In that issue's article announcing Miller's return to *Daredevil*, he said, "I looked at the way Daredevil's become increasingly despondent and has picked up an edge of paranoid and realized that here was a man who was headed for a breakdown! I'll be bringing Daredevil's dark side into focus. Although I'll be taking what Denny's done and using it to delineate the character, Daredevil's mental collapse can be traced back to my last issue, #191, and to his personality flaws from issue number one."

Miller did at least end with a potentially positive note for the character somewhere down the line: "An enormous positive character will emerge from this." But that rebirth would not come easily.

That magazine's bare description of what was coming only stated that Miller "plans on taking the Man Without Fear in completely new directions, including taking away his 'yuppie-philanthropist' lifestyle." Miller said, "He'll be dirt-poor," and added that he would explore further the relationship between Daredevil and the Kingpin, who "will be the 'main players' on the book."

And then, in August 1985, *The Comics Journal* #101 featured additional quotes from Miller on what was coming: "Every aspect of [Murdock's] life is going to change, including what he does for a living." He added that "Daredevil's secret identity would be revealed to the Kingpin, and as a result, Matt Murdock's life will be 'demolished.' He won't have the security he once did as a lawyer in his 20s."

Which may have all come to pass, yet none of these surface descriptions would properly prepare *Daredevil* readers for what was coming.

2

The Creative Team Dynamic

David Mazzucchelli began penciling *Daredevil* with issue #206. *Daredevil* was his first continuous run on a comic series, and the artistic growth he displayed by the time he started "Born Again," barely two years later, was astounding.

Mazzucchelli, born in 1960, was a graduate of the Rhode Island School of Design. He got his first Marvel assignment at age 23, and was only 24 when he took over *Daredevil*. Mazzucchelli's pencils showed dynamism from his first issue, and also echoes of previous *Daredevil* artists, notably the fluid action sequences and character poses of Gil Kane, and also Miller himself. At the start, Mazzucchelli only penciled the series, with finishes provided by inkers such as Danny Bulanadi, Pat Redding, Kim DeMulder, and others.

Mazzucchelli's first issue also displayed a unique flair for background detail, as well as an emphatic use of light and shadow to accentuate the emotions in any given scene. For a neophyte comic-book artist, he also displayed a veteran's comfort with well-choreographed action scenes.

When Mazzucchelli began inking his own pencils in *Daredevil* #214, it was clear that Mazzucchelli was a rare talent, capable of emphasizing particular moods, with characters' emotions playing out across their faces even while in the middle of brutal fight scenes.

For all of his rapid development as an artist in his first two years on the title, it was his pairing with writer Frank Miller— working from full scripts, not from Miller's layouts, as Klaus Janson did toward the end of Miller's first stint on *Daredevil*— that gave him the perfect partner and storyline to emphasize his many strengths. In fact, the Miller and Mazzucchelli team produced two seminal works together during this period, the other a four-issue miniseries for DC Comics, *Batman: Year One*.

But that seminal work was preceded by "Born Again," which is where the team first displayed all they had to offer through this unique creative partnership.

The storyline that became known as "Born Again" began in *Daredevil* #227, but all the groundwork for what was to follow was laid in the previous issue, in which Miller returned as co-writer alongside outgoing scribe Denny O'Neil. Mazzucchelli's pencils in that issue were inked by Dennis Janke, whose delicate line work lessened the shadows and the mood on display in the prior issues' pages inked by Mazzucchelli. But even with this partial pairing of Miller and Mazzuchelli, the first page of *Daredevil* #227, the kick-off of "Born Again," would blow minds and energize readers as much as any previous Miller-helmed issue.

Describing both Mazzucchelli's talent and their collaborative process for "Born Again" in the article in *Marvel Age* #36, Miller said, "You'll be seeing David come on strong as one of the best artists in years. He's smart, energetic, and can draw better and more powerfully issue by issue! All the while, his work has a sense of joy to it, of the Stan Lee-Gene Colan *Daredevil* [of the mid-1960s]."

In the *Marvel Age* feature, Miller added, "I write [scripts] like letters to David, throwing him problems. I have yet to see a panel in the *Daredevil*s we've done where David failed to find an intelligent, dramatic solution, one that emphasizes the humanity of the scene. He's a very down-to-earth, expressive artist."

About their collaboration, Mazzucchelli added, "When I first came on the series, I was very aware of the mark Frank had made and it was very much in my mind not to do the same thing he had done. [But] I culled what I could from the history of the book and made it my own. Sometimes as I'm reading a script, an image pops into my head of how Frank Miller would do it, and then I think about how David Mazzucchelli would do it."

The way they did it together over the course of this series would produce memorable, lasting, and important work. "Born Again" was about to change everything for the character and the title itself.

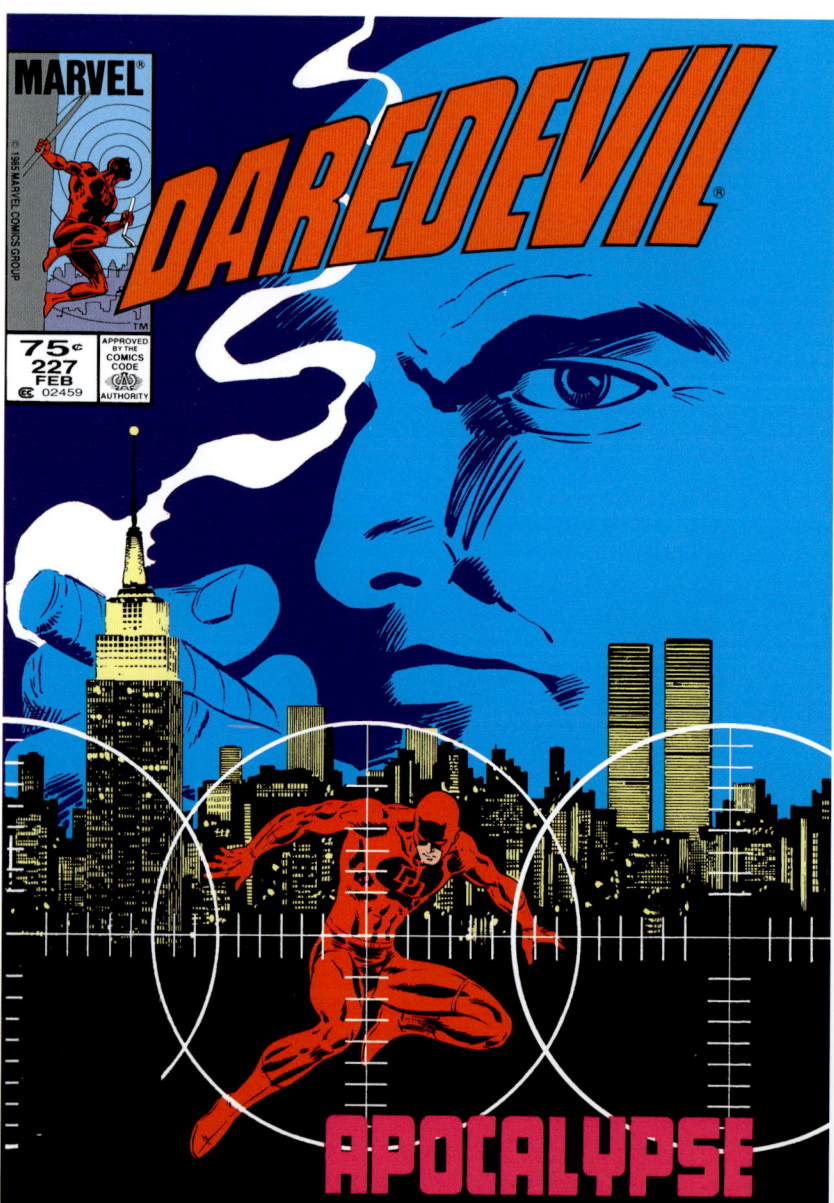

3

Born Again

Chapter One: "Apocalypse"

When *Daredevil #227* opens in that dusty motel room in a scene diffuse with pale yellow light streaming in through louvered blinds, readers are hit with multiple sensations: The room is too cramped, the environment too hot, and the character at the center of the scene is radiating desperate need. This was an atypical start to a super hero comic. Immediately, readers were dropped into a compelling scene full of dread potent.

Karen Page sits slumped on a chair in a dingy motel room in Mexico; her circumstances are unknown to us but obviously she is in turmoil. This fact alone is jarring to readers who knew Karen as Matt Murdock's first girlfriend introduced in his first issue, a sunny blonde office assistant who brought light into the always dark world of the blind

Matt Murdock. And that was how she remained until her last appearance in the series nearly one hundred issues prior.

With Karen Page, as was the case with so many of Matt Murdock's loves, his secret identity as Daredevil would drive a wedge between them. But Page as we knew her was bright and positive, someone who aspired to leave Matt Murdock and New York and head west to seek her fortunes as an actor in Hollywood.

Only, as *Daredevil* #227 displayed from its first page, the reality was much more dire than her aspirations. Page, seen here with her face half in shadow, her hair unkempt, and her body language that of someone defeated by hardship, is not living the Hollywood dream at all. In fact, she's about as far from it as she can be. As the narration tells us, "It's not every day you sell your soul."

And it's not just her soul that Karen is selling: We learn in this opening scene that Karen Page is a junkie, in the throes of heroin withdrawal and in desperate need of satisfying the chemical hunger gnawing at her. Her character hasn't thrived in California like readers assumed she would when she left eight years earlier. Indeed, her acting career evolved to the point where readers learn that she's been making "stag films" as her addiction grew. She is far removed from the life she once knew and the career she intended.

Broke in finances and spirit, Karen sells off what she thinks is the only remaining object of value that she owns: Matt Murdock's secret identity.

Over the years, as Murdock and Page's relationship developed, it followed the usual comic-book contrivance of Murdock using pretty much any means to keep her from learning his secret. But eventually she did, and together or apart, that secret was something she protected for a long time.

Until now.

Until she sold her former lover's secret super-hero identity for a fix.

Now, keep in mind, this dire and desperate scene plays out on just the first page of this first issue.

Upon the page-turn, that foreboding opening scene full of wan yellows and smoky blacks, courtesy of colorist Christie Scheele, shifts to one diffuse with deep, fiery reds, as Daredevil's secret identity is passed in a sealed envelope from assorted underworld figures until it is finally handed to the person who will become the architect of Daredevil's demise—as well as perhaps his own—the Kingpin of Crime.

Throughout his appearances in Marvel's titles from the mid-1960s to the late 1970s, the Kingpin was portrayed as a somewhat cartoonish gangster figure, an immense form clad in purple striped pants and a white jacket, and toting a cane that fired beams of energy. His sheer size made him a good foil for his frequent antagonist Spider-Man, but it also meant the character was subject to plenty of quips about his size, too. He was dangerous but rarely treated as an overly serious threat.

Until Miller brought him into *Daredevil* during his previous time guiding the series. From his first appearance in Miller's initial run, starting with only his second issue as writer, the Kingpin became an imposing presence, as a physical threat but also as a controlling force behind the scenes, directing the New York underworld and employing a steady string of personal assassins to do his bidding.

Daredevil and the Kingpin were at odds from the start, a situation that seemed inevitable considering Daredevil's crime-fighting penchant as well as his day job as one charged with upholding the law. Although it was also that dichotomy that led to their relationship occasionally turning toward helping one another … if Matt Murdock felt the means justified the end for the moment, anyway.

When last Miller wrote the Kingpin in an issue of *Daredevil*, in his penultimate issue, #190, it was a more helpful Kingpin who led Daredevil to a resurrection ceremony featuring poor, then-deceased Elektra. Never mind the fact that it was the Kingpin's assassin Bullseye who originally killed her under Fisk's orders. In this case, helping Daredevil meant also helping himself, as Daredevil cut through the ninja organization the Hand that was cutting into the Kingpin's action. At the dénouement of the issue, after Elektra was herself born again, unbeknownst to Matt, Kingpin reminded Daredevil that "We need each other, Daredevil. We are **partners** after a fashion. We are the **power** in this city."

As of *Daredevil* #227, that loose partnership came to a crashing halt.

Kingpin first appears in the issue on the deck of a cruise ship, wearing not his usual natty gangster attire but what could instead be comical cruise-ship attire in the wrong artistic hands: He's seen sporting an unbuttoned short-sleeved shirt covering a T-shirt stretched across his prodigious midsection, clad in elastic shorts and wearing flip-flops. An outfit hardly designed to strike fear into the hearts of his enemies.

But so adept is the Mazzucchelli and Scheele art team that the outfit is somehow even more terrifying than Kingpin's usual work clothes. Seen at a low angle, the background of the page awash in dark reds and purples, the Kingpin has rarely looked more imposing. The page serves as a reminder that the clothing isn't what makes the man, it's the absolute immorality and implacable approach to his work that has kept him in his supreme position among other underworld figures.

Handed the envelope that he's told contains Daredevil's true identity, Kingpin's reaction is calm, measured, and all the more chilling.

"Locate everyone who has **touched** this envelope -- or spoken to anyone who **has** -- and await the **kill order**."

And then things get worse.

Three pages into the issue, it's clear that bad times are ahead for Matt Murdock. Especially when the page ends with a simple caption mentioning a time-jump: "Six months pass." Six months of Kingpin holding onto such privileged information. He didn't use this information in a rash, impulsive way, confronting Murdock or forcing a physical confrontation in front of loved ones. No, the Kingpin as we're re-introduced to him here is a true gangster, but also a smart, patient, and methodical one.

The story turns then to Matt Murdock, seen from overhead on a splash page that announces the issue's title. It's a scene that should come across as calming: Murdock is seen from above, asleep in his bed inside his ritzy New York brownstone. But he doesn't look to be at rest at all. As portrayed by Mazzucchelli, Murdock looks like his sleep has been restless. The tangle of sheets and blanket around him look messy and unkempt, like he has tossed and turned all night.

WINTER HITS MANHATTAN LIKE AN UNWANTED RELATIVE. DROPS IN WITH NO WARNING AND SEEMS TO STAY FOREVER.

IT SPREADS A THICK WHITE BLANKET THAT MAKES THE CITY LOOK CLEAN FOR A FEW HOURS-- UNTIL THE SNOW GETS STEPPED ON AND DRIVEN OVER AND MADE GRITTY AND DIRTY GREY.

MATT MURDOCK IS BLIND--SO HE MISSES THE PRETTIEST MORNING OF THE YEAR. ALL HE GETS IS HISSING PIPES AND AN EAST COAST CHILL THAT GOES STRAIGHT FOR THE BONES.

MATT MURDOCK IS ALSO DAREDEVIL.

THAT'S WHY HIS LIFE IS ABOUT TO FALL APART.

Stan Lee presents

APOCALYPSE

By FRANK MILLER AND DAVID MAZZUCCHELLI

CHRISTIE SCHEELE
COLORS

JOE ROSEN
LETTERS

RALPH MACCHIO
EDITOR

JIM SHOOTER
EDITOR IN CHIEF

Of course, it's likely not helpful in creating a placid scene that across the bottom-third of the page is the issue's title—"Apocalypse"—presented in thick letters awash with flaming yellows and oranges.

Mazzucchelli's art, his choice of the overhead camera angle, and the blend of an unsettled Matt Murdock alongside captions that build the tension even before the character wakes is a perfect example of how well Miller and Mazzucchelli are in sync right from the start, despite this being the first full issue they worked on together.

Miller's captions throughout this issue and the series are terse, owing more to hard-boiled detective fiction than the usual sorts of thoughts running around a character's head in a comic book. It's an approach Miller employed more and more after this series, most notably on *Batman: Year One* and then his crime-noir series *Sin City*, but rarely has he used this technique to such emotionally charged effect as he does across these seven issues.

Put another way, the review magazine *Comics Feature Presents Super-Heroes* #1 stated that "Miller's return [features] some of the finest writing to ever grace a comic-book page. Clearly inspired by film noir, hard-boiled detective thrillers and sheer commitment to portraying genuine human conflict, Miller's writing is so unique in comic books that, once again, it was almost impossible for anyone to follow."

Another repeating motif first seen here, but echoed in increasingly dire ways across the subsequent issues that display Murdock's collapse, is the overhead view that starts out showing a Matt Murdock at least able to have restless sleep in the comfort of his own home before his downward spiral becomes fully evident.

But for now, as restless and unsettled as he feels, he still wakes up inside the comfortable and spacious confines of the well-to-do lawyer that he is. For now.

Murdock is out of bed and feeling unsettled, but after all he's been through of late personally and professionally, it doesn't occur to him that this feeling might presage something even worse on the horizon. Mazzucchelli and Scheele portray Murdock's home as well-lit and secure against the view outside his windows, where they remove all black lines and use icy blue color holds to really emphasize the winter chill outside his windows. Murdock is well-protected from outside forces.

Then his life falls apart, not through the kind of apocalypse we might expect in a super hero comic, but rather in much more mundane and frightening way: with a pile of envelopes shoved through the mail slot in his front door. Letters that tell him his mortgage payments never showed up and other such payments are also in arrears; there's an audiotape from his girlfriend, Glorianna O'Breen, breaking up with him. And none of the job offers a lawyer of his caliber might have expected to find amidst the other mail.

A knock at his door reveals a process server handing him a subpoena. It seems that Nick Manolis, a police lieutenant who has worked with Daredevil numerous times and always proven to be an upstanding cop, has given a sworn statement saying that Matt Murdock perjured himself in a recent case. Murdock knows it isn't true, but he's still summoned to appear and face the charges anyway.

Without once facing a super-powered villain or even donning his red costume—all before his morning coffee, in fact—Murdock's relatively comfortable life has been devastated, his personal finances and professional circumstances both suddenly as dire as can be.

By the afternoon, Matt's finances are frozen and his girlfriend has broken up with him without giving him a chance to defend himself. So it's hard to blame him for having paranoid thoughts that the world is conspiring against him, especially considering his already fractious mental state. But because the challenges he's contending with are either bureaucratic or personal (and his own fault, in the case of Glori), it doesn't occur to Matt that maybe something more is going on. That maybe someone, somewhere, is carefully orchestrating his systematic downfall.

Meanwhile, Glorianna O'Breen is also in a fragile state, but not over her failed relationship with Matt Murdock. When readers meet her in this issue, it's after she has returned to her apartment to find it had been burgled, her furniture and personal possessions strewn everywhere. The way Mazzucchelli portrays the chaos in her apartment dwellings is a suitable physical manifestation of the emotional storm that her recent time with Murdock has brought into her life. She needs some kind of anchor, and so of course, into this scene comes the ever-friendly shoulder to cry on, Matt's ex-partner Foggy Nelson, who provides the lift that Glori needs.

After the morning he had, Matt Murdock is in a spiral, so confides in *Daily Bugle* reporter Ben Urich, a seasoned reporter who once sussed out Matt Murdock's secret identity and then buried the story to protect the city's champion in Daredevil. Along with likely passing on the Pulitzer Prize-worthy story of the blind hero's costumed adventures, Urich's association with Murdock led to the reporter being threatened, attacked, and very nearly murdered by Elektra.

Urich wants to help but finds all such offers of assistance rebuffed by Murdock in a concerning way.

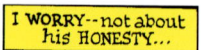

A note about Ben Urich: As much as "Born Again" is focused on the fall and rise of Matt Murdock, it also becomes Ben Urich's story, too. Urich, a cynical, middle-aged reporter, is as close as the reader has to an everyman in this tale. Foggy Nelson is another, certainly, but there's something about Foggy's air of endless, somewhat clueless, positivity that keeps him in a protective bubble even as Murdock's life turns to chaos around him. Urich is too world-weary and sharp-eyed a reported to miss the kinds of details that fail to penetrate Foggy's sunny veneer until it's too late.

Ben Urich barely recognizes Murdock's voice on the call, in such a bad way is Murdock already. Urich saw the reports about Matt's supposed wrongdoing and doesn't believe it, but when he starts to question Matt about it, Murdock's only reply is that of a stranger: "I have no statement for the press." The phone goes dead. And Urich sits, worried, as Mazzucchelli's expert use of shadows in the late-night newsroom threatens to envelop Urich even more.

Matt, under threat of foreclosure and beset by additional financial problems ("…I hate money…" he thinks), tries to find solace as Daredevil. As he changes into the costume and heads out into the night, he thinks, "Something loose and wild flows through the city. I feel my pulse quicken… it's the night. I've always loved it." His time as Daredevil, he thinks, is "the only part of my life worth living any more. It's the one relief I can give myself… when it all gets to be too much."

This would be the last time for multiple issues to follow that appearing as Daredevil brings him any joy or relief at all.

Meanwhile, Foggy Nelson and Glorianna O'Breen are warming up inside his apartment. Mazzucchelli's art communicates volumes to readers as the two friends sit, their casual closeness and relaxed facial expressions are bathed in the warm glow of the fireplace light, expertly illuminating their growing comfort with one another.

Meanwhile, while his friends are warm, Matt Murdock is cold and alone in icy New York, as he attempts to meet his situation head-on. He breaks into Lieutenant Manolis' house and confronts him about the lies the cop has been telling about Matt Murdock. Following a brief, if futile, physical response by Manolis, Murdock leaves, but stays close enough that his enhanced hearing allows him to listen in on the call the desperate Manolis makes a moment later. He reports that Daredevil did indeed show up at his apartment, but also mentions treatment that his sick son desperately needs.

Murdock can't hear the voice on the other end of the call but at least he now knows: Someone is out to get Matt Murdock. He returns home, finds his electricity and phone disconnected, and drops into an even more restless sleep.

Foggy and Glorianna enjoyed a chaste night together, but when his phone rings and she picks up, it's Matt who's calling. He wonders if he misdialed. But there's no time to dwell on Glori being at his friend's house so early in the morning, so he ignores that and instead tells Foggy he needs his help—he's been summoned before a grand jury.

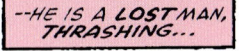

--HE IS A *LOST MAN,* THRASHING...

From there, readers and the Kingpin both have a front seat to Murdock's decline. Kingpin, through a series of photographs and reports from his minions, observes, as one caption reads, "a stop-motion study of Murdock's deterioration." Murdock spends his days in court with Foggy, trying to prove his innocence. His nights are even more desperate, as his costumed alter-ego grows increasingly violent, culminating in a public episode in a waterfront saloon where his violent thrashing is on full display.

As the Kingpin looks on from the comfort of his nerve center, a look of grim satisfaction crosses his face. He's confident that his meticulous plan has systematically destroyed his enemy's career, character, and now perhaps even his sanity.

He also takes notice of Foggy Nelson's courtroom prowess, making a note to have him hired, which is just one more way Kingpin commodifies "lesser" men. Nelson and Murdock, attorneys-at-law, might have bedeviled him in the past but if he can use one while also aiming to destroy the other, all the better.

Everything is going more perfectly than Kingpin could have hoped. Foggy does help Matt Murdock avoid prison time, but he is disbarred and left broke. Kingpin has succeeded in stripping the law from his enemy's life. He's satisfied with the destructive results of his plan.

Or is he?

Even as he savors this victory, Kingpin remains intrigued by Murdock. He knows he should stop now and leave Murdock to the added misery that awaits his every waking day from here on out. He must, as he tells himself, "**deny** myself the exquisite pleasure of a killing **stroke**…"

While Matt Murdock's life is falling apart, the catalyst for that collapse, Karen Page, is nearly murdered herself, as the Kingpin's kill order has finally reached her. She manages to escape, fleeing for her life and hating herself for the one name that comes to her as she does, "the man who **always** helped-- **Matt**--"

Unfortunately, Matt's problems are all-consuming at the moment. He's down to his final thirty dollars, he's unemployed, and increasingly convinced that everyone from Con Ed to Glorianna, and maybe even Foggy, despite all his efforts to help Matt in court, are out to get him.

Matt is exhausted, his paranoia growing. He heads home to get much-needed sleep.

He's only steps from the door to his brownstone when it explodes in a silent, terrible, but beautiful sequence by Mazzucchelli that is painted in crimson and yellow. Literal pieces of his former life land at Murdock's feet. His home is destroyed. There's nothing left. Nothing, except…

In the rubble, Murdock finds the one item that survived the destruction.

His Daredevil costume.

He falls to his knees amidst the rubble, tears streaming down his face.

He now *knows*. He knows that "nothing about it said **gangster** until this."

Chapter Two: "Purgatory"

When "Born Again" began, the cover to *Daredevil* #227 didn't clue the reader in that they were in for a one-of-a-kind Daredevil story. The issue is striking in its way, with Daredevil in the foreground in the center of the Kingpin's crosshairs while, in the background, Wilson Fisk's visage looms large over the New York skyline. It was nicely rendered but nothing out of the ordinary, contents-wise.

But the second chapter's cover was striking for the fact that it doesn't show the costumed title character at all. In fact, Matt Murdock-as-Daredevil would be absent from the next few covers (outside of the corner box art, anyway). *Daredevil* #228's cover features a too-close image of Matt Murdock's face, his frantic and sweat-beaded visage split down the middle by fracture lines, resulting in half his face being offset from the rest. His fractured psyche given physical form.

The issue opens on a scene of relative bliss, as Matt's former friend and lover, Foggy and Glorianna, play at domesticity in an attempt to not worry about the now-missing Matt. And because, more and more, they are enjoying each other's company on a more romantically inclined level.

This placid scene is interrupted by a phone call. Glori picks up and while readers aren't privy to the caller's words, it doesn't matter because the shock registering on her face says it all. Troubled, she tells Foggy, "--it was **Matt**--and he dinna make any **sense**--"

She didn't know the half of it.

The issue's title splash page again shows us Matt Murdock from an overhead view. Only this time, he's not asleep in his own bed. No, for chapter two's "Purgatory," Murdock is inside a tiny, dingy motel, curled up on a twin bed with rickety frame, the room barely wide enough to accommodate the bed, a radiator, and a tiny dresser. The thin rug on the floor is peeling away; likewise, the paint on the walls.

Murdock's narration as he wakes in that run-down motel portrays a man still in some command of his faculties. At the same time, distraught and alone with his thoughts, he drifts deeper into paranoia, convinced that everyone is out to get him. Companies, friends, former lovers.

Reason tries to assert itself, as he reminds himself that his old nemesis the Kingpin is to blame for his situation. Somehow Kingpin learned that Murdock is Daredevil, and used that information to destroy his life. Murdock also convinces himself that there's only one way to get his life back—he has to go to the Kingpin and kill him.

The reasonable part of him knows he can't do that, that it's wrong. But maybe beating him until he promises to give Murdock back his life is okay... and then he sleeps and dreams of killing the Kingpin. Fantasizing about how doing so will give him his life back.

Waking, he has no sense of what time it is so, as his narration tells us, he calls the time operator. Only what he actually did was call Foggy and Glori again, this time eliciting anguished tears from Glori before Foggy grabs the phone. Where he hears Matt say only, "I'm **on** to you, Nelson."

THE WINDOW'S CLOSED-- BUT YOU'D NEVER KNOW IT, NOT WITH THE STIFF BREEZE THAT'S BLOWING THROUGH IT, GIVING ME A SWEETHEART OF A CRAMP IN MY LOWER BACK.

SIX INCHES OF SNOW OUTSIDE AND STILL NO HEAT IN THE ROOM...

AND HERE I'D PLANNED ON STAYING AT THE PLAZA. THAT WAS BEFORE I DISCOVERED THAT THE IRS HAD MADE MY CREDIT CARDS SO MUCH WORTHLESS PLASTIC.

LEFT ME WITH TEN BUCKS TO MY NAME.

I FOUND A HOTEL THAT MADE CHANGE.

Stan Lee presents

PURGATORY

By FRANK MILLER and DAVID MAZZUCCHELLI

R. LEWIS	JOE ROSEN	RALPH MACCHIO	JIM SHOOTER
COLORS	LETTERS	EDITOR	EDITOR IN CHIEF

The motel's schlubby manager gets it worse. He arrives at Murdock's room to remind him of the check-out time and is quickly beaten into unconsciousness after Murdock, in his fevered paranoia, convinces himself that the man sent by the Kingpin.

And then he decides it's time to take the fight to the Kingpin after all.

As he makes his way to the Kingpin's building, one of the gangster's men has been watching. He reports back to his boss on Murdock's ever-more-worrisome mental state.

Murdock rides the subway en route to the Kingpin's high-rise, sitting unmoving, his expression implacable behind mirrored sunglasses, even when armed criminals rob the other passengers. It's jarring to see this former staunch defender of all people in his city sit and do nothing at all while the other subway-riders are attacked right next to him.

It's only when the violence threatens him personally that he takes drastic and brutal action, first against the criminals and then by beating a police officer who happens upon the scene. Murdock takes the cop's nightstick and heads toward the Kingpin's office.

The Kingpin savors every bit of these details, knowing that Murdock's destination can only be to come after him.

On a public pay phone, Murdock has, we think, a moment of clarity as he calls Foggy and confesses that he knows something is wrong with him, that he's sick. The voice Murdock hears on the other end encourages him to press on, to kill the Kingpin, and put an end to this. Murdock says okay, he'll give it his best shot.

Then he drops the phone's receiver and we "hear" the voice on the other end: the robot voice of the time operator. Chilling stuff.

The action then switches from the snowy cold of New York to the sweltering heat of South America, as Karen Page, still on the run from the Kingpin's assassins, tries to call Matt Murdock, only it seems his number has been disconnected. She knows Matt wouldn't willingly move out of his brownstone. Something must be wrong. But that will have to wait, since the Kingpin's assassins are still in active pursuit.

As Murdock enters the Kingpin's building, reporter Ben Urich sits in another building and frets over Matt Murdock's fate. He *knows* Murdock was framed. He demands that his publisher let him look into this further.

Murdock is welcomed into the Kingpin's office and led into the private gym where the Kingpin stands, waiting. No words are exchanged, nor any needed, as Murdock strikes first. But he has got no strength left. The Kingpin savagely tears into him, relishing the infliction of physical damage on Murdock as much as he did the earlier financial carnage he helped bring about.

The Kingpin wants to take the fight to its ultimate conclusion—he can barely restrain himself from beating the blind hero to death—but is a careful man. Murdock's demise can't be so obvious.

Instead, he orders Murdock's body be doused in alcohol and seatbelted into a taxi cab—its driver beaten to death by Murdock's stolen billy club—and then has the taxi driven off the pier into the East River.

As the Kingpin ruminates in vivid detail about these elements when they're relayed to him, Mazzucchelli shows us the scene itself: a wrecked taxi sitting askew on the trash-filled bottom of the murky East River, its gray-green water more disturbing than the blackness of a grave. Especially when the Kingpin's thoughts focus on what surely must have been the case when Murdock finally woke at the bottom of the river: trapped in the car, its doors sealed shut, with no way to free himself and the awareness that his demise was imminent. That he had no way out. This pleases the Kingpin.

And then, weeks later, the cab is discovered and removed from the river. Photos of the scene are sent to the Kingpin, who looks out through the great glass windows of his impregnable fortress of an office building, the city painted in reds and pinks below. He is given reports and photos showing what must have been a great struggle in the sunken cab. Murdock's blood; a shattered windshield; a safety belt severed by broken windshield glass in what had to have been a terrible effort. The last throes of a dying man.

Only, in a point effectively made, and then repeated, in a panel overlaying an extreme close-up of the Kingpin's eyes, his irises glowing red, "there is no **corpse**."

The issue ends on a silent splash page, in a darkened alley filled with refuse and street-dwellers. Standing among them, dripping dirty water and bathed in shadows too black for us to make out his ragged features, is the barely on his feet—but *alive*—Matt Murdock.

Chapter Three: "Pariah!"

For *Daredevil* #229, Matt Murdock again appears on the cover rather than his titular costumed alter-ego. In this case, a bowed—but not broken—Matt Murdock stares down a knife-wielding man dressed in a Santa Claus suit. And this time, not even the separate corner box art shows the hero in all his costumed glory; instead, the smaller inset image shows a silhouetted figure mirroring the pose from the previous issue's final page—the darkened figure stooped and dripping wet, using the very panel borders to remain shakily on his feet. The message is clear— the trauma Matt faced in the previous two chapters ain't over yet.

The issue opens on a close-up image of a small portion of Matt Murdock's face, his eyes closed, his skin scratched and bloodied. As he dozes—asleep? Unconscious? Near death?— the captions portraying his interior monologue reflect on the childhood accident that cost him his sight while enhancing his remaining senses. Mazzucchelli's art in these few flashback panels is sparse, airy yet gritty. But then the panels go black, along with Matt's eyesight, and remain that way for a few pages.

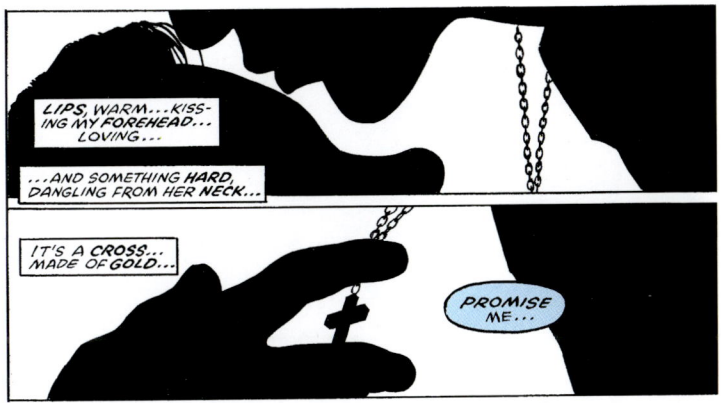

Matt's fractured thoughts replay those early days in the hospital, as his now-uncontrollable, radioactively enhanced senses cause him agony during visits from hospital staff, his single father, and…one other. A woman, gentle and nurturing, offering him comforting words and blessings.

Around her neck, young Matt finds, is a necklace with a pendant—a crucifix.

Matt Murdock wakes in even more dire straits than we last saw him. Again seen from overhead, an even more desperate variation of Murdock is curled up ball-tight on the ground in a garbage-strewn alleyway alongside two other transients. Matt is, as the issue title states in shaky, horror-movie-like block letters, a "Pariah."

...I KEEP MY HEIGHTENED SENSES *SECRET*...EVEN FROM *DAD*...

...I FIND A *TEACHER* WHO HELPS ME *MASTER* THEM...

...AND *DAD* IS *MURDERED* AND I BECOME *DAREDEVIL* AND FIGHT *CRIME*...

...AND *OTHER* THINGS HAPPEN. A *HOME*. A *CAREER*...

...BUT THE *OTHER* THINGS ARE *GONE* NOW SO THEY DON'T *MATTER*...

...*GONE*...THE *KINGPIN* TOOK THEM AWAY. FOUND OUT MY *SECRET* IDENTITY AND TOOK *EVERYTHING* AWAY...

...AND *I ATTACKED* HIM...

...AND HE *KILLED ME.*

Stan Lee
presents

PARIAH!

by FRANK MILLER and DAVID MAZZUCCHELLI

CHRISTIE SCHEELE
COLORS

JOE ROSEN
LETTERS

RALPH MACCHIO
EDITOR

JIM SHOOTER
EDITOR IN CHIEF

It's Christmastime in New York. Matt's former friends, Foggy and Glorianna, fully coupled up now, shop for holiday gifts and are attacked by a mugger. Foggy fends the man off with a bowling ball but not in time to prevent Glori's disillusionment with the city from growing greater still.

Reporter Ben Urich, meanwhile, goes to visit Nick Manolis in the hospital, where the cop whose lies helped bring down Matt Murdock is sitting with his terminally ill child and an ill-tempered nurse.

Mazzucchelli's scenes with Ben Urich start move away from his naturalistic approach and instead take on a more angular, somewhat distorted look that showcases the continued evolution of the artist's style but also helps further emphasize the personal drama Urich is experiencing as he learns more about Murdock's fate, a situation that will soon intertwine the two men once again. Mazzucchelli's gaunt, starkly expressioned Ben Urich knows the cop Manolis lied about Matt Murdock, and now Manolis knows he knows.

Murdock, waterlogged and suffering but on his feet, stumbles onto a snowy New York street, where he's struck by a car, breaking some ribs. And then, for good measure, he gets stabbed in his stomach by a familiar low-level criminal foil who he used to easily handle in his Daredevil guise.

Staggering and bleeding profusely, nearly bowled over from pain and from the damage to his body, Murdock continues to stumble forward, determined to stay upright. He keeps moving because he knows he has to.

Events accelerate in the wrong direction for those in his radius: Manolis' son dies, and after his loss, he no longer has the energy or the motivation to deny Urich's questions. He's ready to confess to his part in the Kingpin's frame job. The two men head out of the hospital to talk, only they're followed by the no-nonsense nurse, who proceeds to beat the hell out of Manolis and then breaks bones in Urich's typing hand, with a threat to break more of them every time he even utters the name "Matt Murdock."

Karen Page, whose face is also seen here in overly angular, heavy-lined fashion, which only adds to her gaunt appearance, has nothing but another piece of herself to sell for both a fix and transport to the United States to find Matt, both of which she feels are the key to her survival. She finds a drug dealer named Paolo who is willing to barter for just such a fee, which he plans to collect in earnest after he kills two of the Kingpin's men who finally tracked her down. At great cost, Karen has someone who will help her get to America and, she hopes desperately, to Matt Murdock.

Only Murdock is currently bleeding out on a desolate Hell's Kitchen street. He stumbles, nearly unconscious, to the place where Daredevil was really "born" as a child, his father's long-shuttered boxing gym.

Matt makes his way inside the gym. Bemoaning his fate and cursing his father, Matt puts all he has into one more punch against the heavy bag hanging in the gym. And then he passes out against it.

He's not alone for long. He's found by a woman in a nun's habit. A woman wearing a cross of gold.

While the entire premise of "Born Again" carries with it certain religious connotations, it's not until the finale of this issue that the implied becomes the explicit: first with the appearance of the nun, a reminder to readers of Matt Murdock's own Catholicism, but then, even more blatantly, the final image of Murdock being held by the unknown nun echoes the poses of Mary cradling Jesus in Michelangelo's masterpiece carving "La Pietà." Mazzucchelli's portrayal of this image with Murdock and the nun is diffuse with warm beams of light cutting through a background of thick, stippled black. It's a tragic end to the issue, if not to Murdock himself, too.

But the issue isn't quite done yet. Even while Murdock and those around him are about at their lowest ebb, the Kingpin isn't quite celebrating his victory yet, either. In this chapter's final page, Kingpin is again working out, covered with sweat, the close-up image of his eyes showing no light or joy over what he's accomplished in tearing down Murdock's life.

Instead, he's tortured by the thoughts that the man he thought he murdered is alive, his hatred growing into obsession. It's here, in this final scene, that we see a moment of weakness in this thus-far unstoppable force. It's also here that Miller's interior monologues, gripping and memorable throughout the issue, reach their apex with an oft-referenced line overlaying an image of the Kingpin's concerned expression that ends the issue. As the Kingpin is discomforted by his train of thought about Murdock surviving all that was thrown at him, one idea especially gnaws at him:

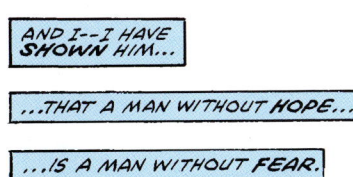

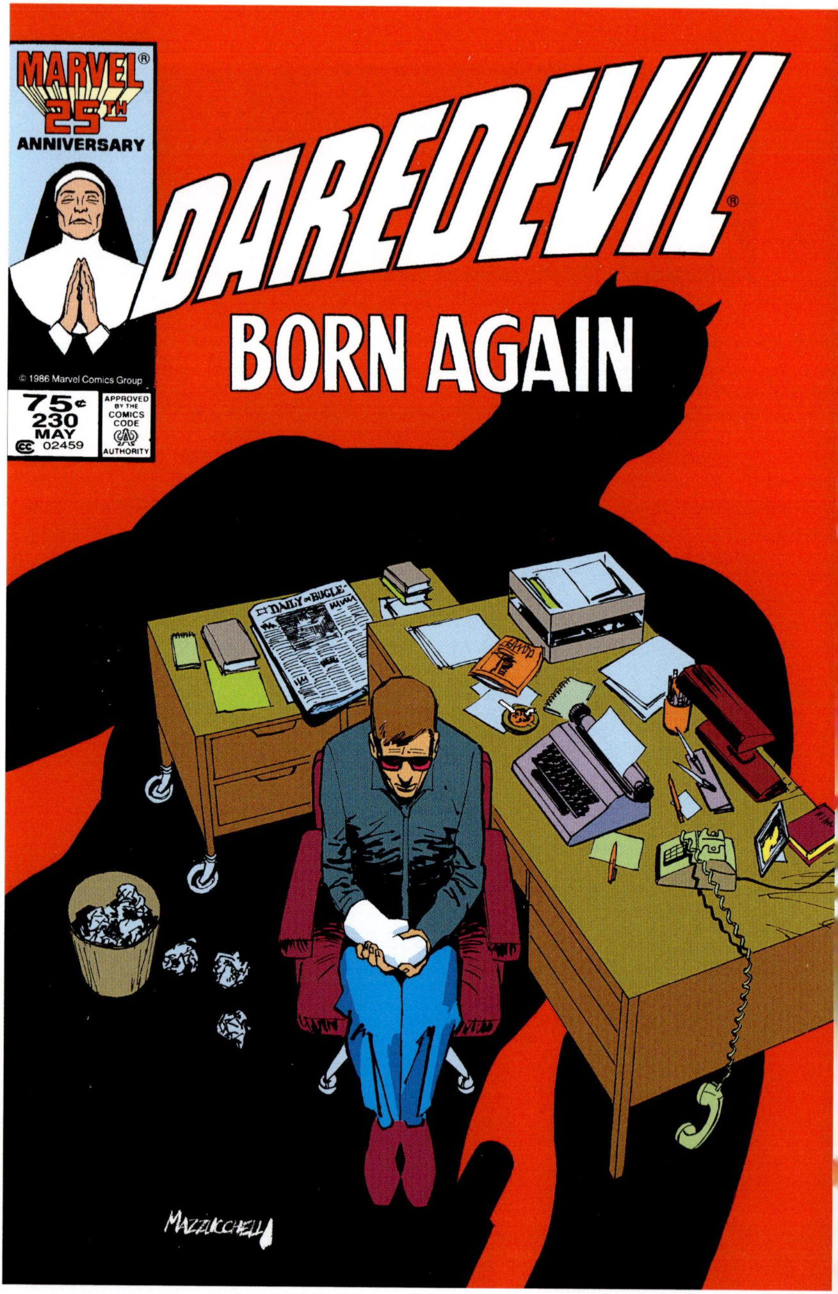

MARVEL ®
25TH
ANNIVERSARY

© 1986 Marvel Comics Group

75¢
230
MAY
CC 02459

APPROVED
BY THE
COMICS
CODE
AUTHORITY

DAREDEVIL ®

BORN AGAIN

MAZZUCCHELLI

Chapter Four: "Born Again"

The cover to *Daredevil* #230 again avoids showcasing a more standard image of the costumed hero. Instead, Mazzucchelli delivers a cover showing a large silhouette of Daredevil casting a shadow over reporter Ben Urich seated in his office chair, his body tightly wound and his expression one of extreme worry.

Mazzucchelli does provide one hopeful visual cue on the cover: The corner box art on this cover replaces the title character entirely with that of the elderly nun we met last issue, her eyes closed and her hands clasped in prayer. The previous three issues, the issues' titles were placed at the bottom of the covers. Here, the subtitle is front and center under the *Daredevil* logo itself:

"Born Again."

Yet, when the issue opens, Matt Murdock is perhaps more near death than he's ever been. Mazzucchelli opens and closes the page in the same way, with thin black panels showing only the thin line of Murdock's heartbeat as though the panels were an EKG machine. That heartbeat line has been reduced to a mere blip. In between the erratic beats, dreamlike panels summarizing the previous few issues help remind readers just how things got so bad. But maybe things are finally taking a positive turn.

Matt Murdock lives! Somehow, despite all he's been through, when we see Murdock awake from that familiar overhead angle, this time Mazzucchelli presents readers with a bearded Matt Murdock, his bare chest bandaged, asleep in a Christlike pose. The nun from the previous issue—Maggie is her name—sits on one side of his mattress. Around them, other sisters of the clergy tend to additional people in need. Finally, Matt Murdock once again knows a degree of shelter.

The Kingpin is frustrated by Murdock's continued survival, but without knowing how to find his enemy, he takes his physical frustrations out on his men during a particularly brutal training session. He also continues to pull apart the life Matt Murdock once knew, as Murdock's former partner Foggy Nelson takes a job at a law firm secretly owned by the Kingpin.

Mazzucchelli uses the overhead camera angle one more time in the issue, as he reintroduces reporter Ben Urich with an overhead image of his own. It's a much grimmer scene: As medics tend to the brutally beaten, unconscious body of Nick Manolis, Urich cradles his busted hand in his lap, heeding the nurse's advice (well, threat) and refusing to allow himself to even think of his missing friend's name.

STAN LEE presents

BORN AGAIN

by FRANK MILLER and DAVID MAZZUCCHELLI

MAX SCHEELE	JOE ROSEN	RALPH MACCHIO	JIM SHOOTER
COLORS	LETTERS	EDITOR	EDITOR IN CHIEF

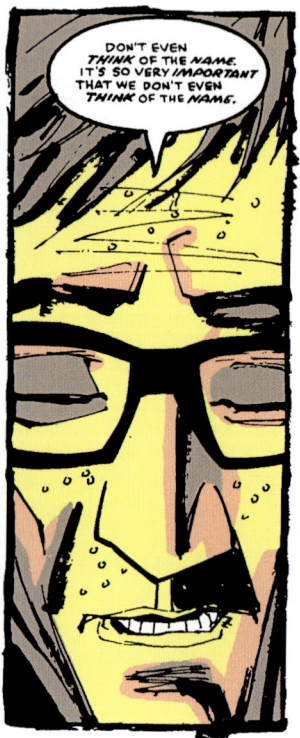

Murdock rests and reflects on his life as it currently exists. With all the other trappings stripped away or destroyed, he's left with only his enhanced senses and one other thing: a drive instilled in him by his poor, doomed boxer of a father to never give up. *Never.*

Mazzucchelli's art in this issue continues to evolve in more angular, often slightly surreal ways. Both story and art are different from where this storyline began, in ways that only enhance the tale being told.

The Kingpin, angry and desperate, orders his consigliere to bring in "Nuke." Nuke is not a familiar name of any Marvel character but the terrifying look on Kingpin's face when he insists on this, er, nuclear option clearly communicates that this person is someone to fear.

Ben Urich, looking wan and diminished, sits in his apartment as his wife frets over the trouble he and Matt Murdock ("don't say the name") have brought into their home. In these scenes, Mazzucchelli's figures get even more stark, the hard, angular lines on Urich's face further emphasizing the anguish he's feeling.

During his slow, fevered recuperation, Matt Murdock reaches outward with his enhanced senses to determine where he is. He's able to tell he's still in Hell's Kitchen, his birthplace. And more—he's in a church basement. He's not out of the woods yet, though—his fever keeps coming back. The nun, Maggie, tends to him as best she can. Around her neck, Murdock notices, hangs a cross made of gold.

Meanwhile, Karen Page has made it back to New York. Unable to shake Paolo, the drug dealer who ferried her back to the city, she nevertheless manages to make a call to Foggy Nelson in hopes that they can meet. And that Foggy can lead her to Matt.

Ben Urich, back at the *Daily Bugle* but tentative about his every move, is reminded by the cleaning crew that the Kingpin is watching. Urich gets dressed down by the paper's publisher, J. Jonah Jameson, in an office awash in scarlet, the silhouette of the office window miniblinds painting both men with deep black stripes of shadow. Urich sits, silent, afraid to carry on with the story about Matt Murdock that he previously insisted on. Jameson is a longtime newspaperman; he knows what must have happened to Urich and he's sickened by Urich's newfound cowardice. Jameson delivers to Urich a reminder of the power newspapers had at the time: "This is **five million readers'** worth of power. It can depose **mayors**. It can destroy **presidents**. And it's been due to get aimed at the **Kingpin** for **years** now. But it needs **you** to **do** it."

Urich sits in the darkness, silent, unable to look Jameson in the eye.

As the scene shifts in time and widens to show the flurry of activity in the broader newsroom, Urich sits at his desk, disaffected by the noise and deadline furor around him.

One curious note about this scene as portrayed by Mazzucchelli: The newsroom is awash with people and desks, reporters and editors. One scene opposite Urich's desk shows a news photographer named Morton getting dressed down by his editor. At least, in the printed comic, it's a photojournalist named Morton. On Mazzucchelli's original art, that character was drawn as none other than Peter Parker, Spider-Man. That was changed along the way, allowing this story to remain in its own corner of the Marvel Universe, untouched by outside forces or heroes (until the storyline's explosive finale, anyway).

Amidst the newsroom hustle, Urich sits disaffected, especially after his phone rings and he hears the voice of the hospitalized Nick Manolis. Manolis is ready to fully confess everything. Urich, fearful and determined to take the Kingpin's minions at their threatening word, refused to engage with Manolis. Nor does he have long to even consider this, since the nurse who broke Urich's hand and beat Manolis enters Manolis' hospital room and finishes the job. Making sure Urich hears every bit of it.

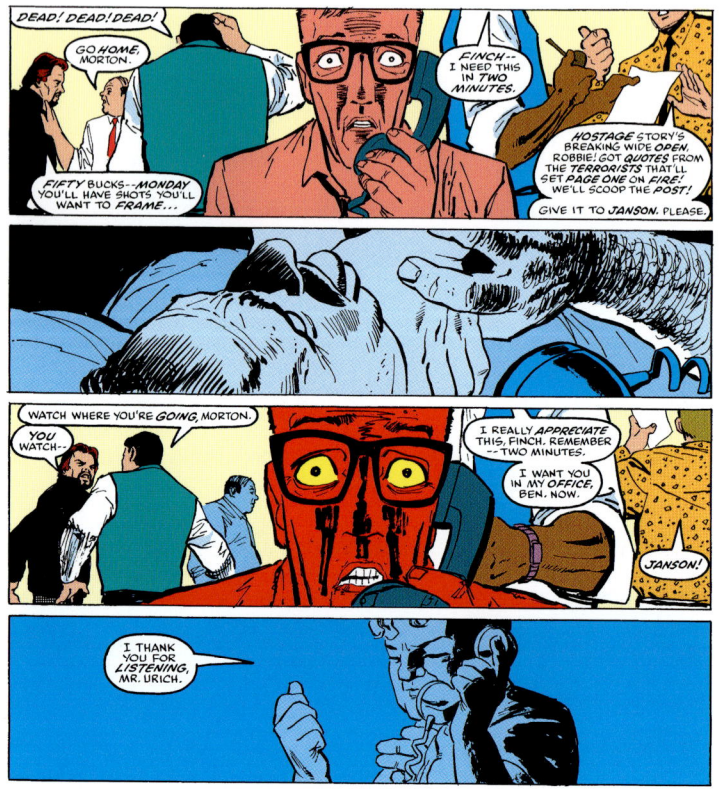

Karen Page and Foggy reunite at a diner, where Foggy tries (and fails) to hide his shock at Karen's emaciated state, and then he fills her in on what he knows about Matt. Which is a fair amount, up til lately, anyway, although he's unaware of Matt's secret identity. Karen, all too aware, knows that Murdock's present situation can only be result of her selling his identity. It's an intense scene, and Mazzucchelli and Scheele bring special focus to the two characters; even as they sit in an otherwise crowded room, they're the only two characters in the world at that moment.

The Kingpin, not content to wait for whoever Nuke is to arrive from out of the country, decides to proactively tear down what little Matt Murdock may still have, if he indeed remains alive: the reputation of Daredevil. So he seeks out a man who "specializes in psychotics," and at the same time strong-arms another former nemesis (turned costume-shop proprietor) of Daredevil's to make a replica of his costume.

Ben Urich sits, alone, terrified, and bitterly aware of what will happen if he continues to investigate the Kingpin; indeed, if he even speaks Daredevil's real name aloud.

He sits, his hand still in cast despite the fact that the doctor has told him the bones had healed. He sits in the cold, feeling scared and unheroic.

But then he removes the cast. His face full of jutting, thick black lines that represent the anguish he feels through every part of his being, he then speaks two words aloud: "**Matt Murdock**." Ben Urich, crime reporter, is born again.

Matt Murdock too has made it through his worst moments and come out the other side. He's awake, sitting in bed, Maggie the nun tending to him once again. His extraordinary senses are getting stronger again, even as he heals. He picks up Maggie's scent—a pleasant one.

So much like my own, he thinks.

"Maggie," Matt asks her, "Are you my **mother**?"

She replies, "Of **course** not, child."

As Matt's enhanced senses remind him, "A **heartbeat** can tell you a **lot**. Hers just **jumped**. She's **lying**."

Chapter Five: "Saved"

Daredevil #231, chapter five of "Born Again," is where things start to get better for some of the characters, but that is still a relative term after what Matt Murdock and the others have been through.

On the cover, Mazzucchelli finally presents readers with an image of a costumed Daredevil… only it's a Daredevil who clearly isn't Matt Murdock, since Matt is also featured on the cover as the recipient of a vicious blow that this "Daredevil" landed on him. The cover reads, in large print against a spare white background stippled with black, "Saved." But neither the larger cover image nor that of the corner box art featuring a squinty eyed Kingpin give the impression that salvation will be quickly attained.

As the issue opens, a re-emboldened Ben Urich is telling his story—Nick Manolis' story, really—to a group of cops even as Matt Murdock punches his way back to health in his father's abandoned gym. And the Kingpin is put on the defensive by his board of directors for letting his personal vendetta overtake his and their business interests. It's all looking promising after some truly harrowing times.

If only that sense of optimism could last.

Urich is assigned a strapping cop as protection, in case his new multi-part exposé of Wilson Fisk's true identity as New York's Kingpin of Crime gets him any blowback. And it most certainly will. In the form of Lois, the nurse who murdered Nick Manolis and broke Urich's hand. Lois is told she's going to be relocated until the current heat on her boss recedes. She doesn't take that news very well and goes to do something about it.

Matt Murdock, back on his feet, may not be ready to re-engage with the people from his old life, but he's begun shadowing them—Ben Urich in particular, since he's not yet aware of Karen Page's desperate return to the city—to make sure the Kingpin's scheme to destroy his life doesn't have further repercussions on his loved ones.

While Matt is stealthily listening to Urich's conversation with the cop, Lois pays a visit to Urich's wife, and then lays in wait for Urich to return home. When he does, Lois brutally assaults Urich's cop bodyguard even as Urich discovers his wife hanging in the shower. Fortunately, she's still alive. While he struggles to free her, there's additional commotion in the other room. Lois is taken down by a silent Matt Murdock, who does his protecting and then disappears. But Urich, returning to the entry way with razor in hand, assuming he'll have to take on Lois himself, instead finds her unconscious alongside the cop. It all starts to sink in for him.

> MATT.

> You're ALIVE.

Costume-maker Melvin Potter has the unfortunate timing of calling Urich's apartment at the conclusion of this attack, wanting to confess to the reporter who has been writing a multi-part Kingpin exposé that he was recently contacted by the Kingpin's men and told to create a Daredevil costume he knows will be used for improper means. Urich, needing to tend to his wife, has no helpful response. But Matt Murdock is still nearby and he too hears Potter's message. He goes to see Potter and, from the shadows, tells him to make the costume, that no one will be hurt. Potter is relieved to know Daredevil is back around, and as Matt Murdock starts performing these positive feats from the sidelines, it's a feeling echoed by the reader. After everything Murdock has been through so far, a harrowing journey that the readers have likewise been on for multiple issues now, it's a comfort to know that the hero, who sccmcd like he truly might not make it back unscathed, is on more secure footing at long last.

Karen Page, the person who currently needs a healthy and heroic Matt Murdock more than anyone else, is busy riding out particularly rough withdrawal symptoms at Foggy Nelson's place. She's at her lowest ebb, wanting a fix... wanting to die. Then she notices out Foggy's window that Paolo, the drug dealer who she escaped from and has been trying to evade, has tracked her to Foggy's.

All of these events are starting to coalesce at a quickening pace.

Melvin Potter delivered the Daredevil costume to the Kingpin's men as directed, and they use it to dress the newly freed "lunatic" that Kingpin ordered, a mute and violently deranged man. What they don't know is that the car they're using to transport this fake Daredevil to Foggy's carries an additional passenger: Matt Murdock, riding atop the vehicle, and listening to every detail of their plan.

Paolo finds Karen. The cops, called by Foggy, find Paolo. The fake Daredevil brutally assaults his handler and then heads toward Foggy's apartment, ready to beat all inhabitants to death with Matt Murdock's own billy club.

Karen realizes that whatever happens to her is one thing, but she needs to spare Foggy, innocent from all of this, from anything worse. She knocks him out and plans to leave, come whatever may with Paolo, if he survives his shootout with the police and with Kingpin's men.

Matt Murdock is in a brutal fight with his costumed alter ego and manages to come out on top, even regaining his old billy club.

Karen Page, on the street, survives Paolo's assault on her, only to have the Kingpin's men arrive on the scene. This results in a firefight between those assassins and Paolo, who is shot but not killed. He urges Karen to grab his gun... but Karen, assuming she won't live to see another day and still deep in the throes of her addiction, instead grabs a drug-filled syringe from inside his coat. She'd prefer to meet her end on her own terms, in the form of one last fix.

Paolo, betrayed, turns his gun on her, aiming to "take you with me, Karen Page." Matt, running along the rooftop, stomps on the edge, causing an icicle to fall and stab Paolo in the arm, knocking the gun out of his hand. Matt then uses his billy club to take out the Kingpin's remaining goon

before he can take the shot. Finally, against all hope, he reunites with Karen in the alleyway amidst a number of unconscious bodies.

Mazzucchelli's final splash page in the issue is a silent one that speaks volumes: He gives us Matt and Karen in the alley, kneeling in the dirty snow, clinging to each other as tears stream down Karen's face.

Readers finally get the payoff of the issue's title. Matt is saved through Karen, and now Karen through Matt. For the moment, both feel hope in each other's arms. For now, both of them are saved,

This concluding scene, showing the syringe in Karen's hand, was only saved by Marvel's willingness to print this particular issue without the approval of the Comics Code Authority (CCA). The CCA was a self-regulating board formed in the mid-1950s and responsible for devising and enforcing a code of ethics and standards as an alternative to proposed government regulation regarding the same. In 2001, Marvel would abandon their adherence to the Comics Code entirely, but at the time of "Born Again's" publication in the mid-1980s, it was still notable for the largest publisher in the country to release a comic without code approval.

In the case of this particular issue, the CCA objected to the appearance of the hypodermic needle in Karen Page's hand—they didn't grok to comics showing drug paraphernalia, a situation which Marvel faced one other time in the past when they ran a multipart drug abuse-related story in *Amazing Spider-Man* without Code approval.

At the conclusion of this fifth chapter, reporter Ben Urich's latest column updates his readers, as well as comic readers, on the dénouement of these many frantic goings-on. The foremost detail of which concerns the escaped asylum inmate who was found unconscious… but without any costume, thereby preserving Daredevil's reputation. Urich's wife lived; many of the other players, like the involved cops and the Kingpin's men, did not.

Through all of this, the issue ends on stark images of Urich against a simple and effective black-and-white dot pattern that echoes newspaper printing, full of resolve: "To find out where Matt Murdock is… and what he has become."

Chapter Six: "God and Country"

Effectively, *Daredevil* #231 was the ending of the "Born Again" storyline. These final two issues of Miller and Mazzucchelli's time on the title are certainly connected to the previous five, but they also expand the storyline in ways far beyond the personal story being told thus far. As such, the entirety of the Miller and Mazzucchelli issues, seven issues in all, have since been compiled under the "Born Again" subtitle (with *Daredevil* #226, the prelude issue co-written by Miller, occasionally collected as an adjunct chapter as well).

While the previous chapters largely told a smaller story involving the Kingpin's deconstruction of a singular hero, and the hero's subsequent attempts to survive and bring himself back to some form of normalcy again, this chapter and the

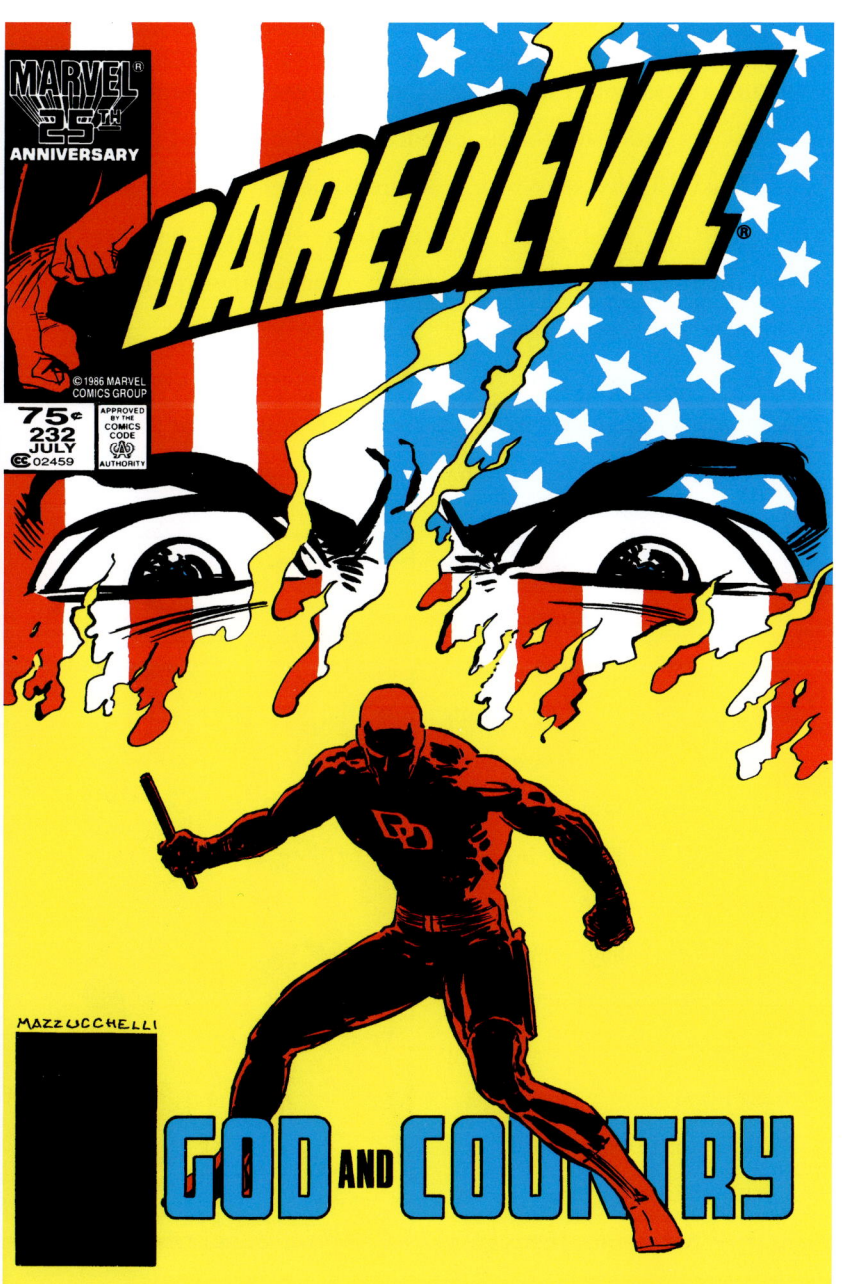

finale in #233 both expand the literal blast radius around these characters and make the series once more a connected part of the Marvel Universe. Which is where some felt the story went awry, getting too big and involving larger-than-life characters like the Avengers in ways that greatly changed the street-level drama of the previous issues.

And yet, seen through the Kingpin's squinty eyes, the increasingly loud and violent extremes he resorted to to take down Matt Murdock emphasized his growing desperation to do so.

This issue's cover image shows the fully costumed hero, his background aflame, and an ominous image of glowering eyes cast down at Daredevil's. Those eyes, rendered in stark black and white, are imposed over the red, white, and blue of the American flag, rendered as color holds, all primary colors with no black lines, to diminish their impact.

The story opens not in New York but instead in a war-torn part of Nicaragua. There, we're introduced to the character sporting the red, white, and blue of the cover—*Nuke*, mentioned in name only in the previous issue. Here, he's dressed like a soldier in a war movie, his blonde hair closely cropped above a face tattooed with the American flag.

Nuke is a Reagan-era monster, a single-minded super-soldier amped up on amphetamines and toting a massive machine gun with a digital readout of the armament the weapon expels. He's confused about where he is, ranting as he does about saving "our boys" from captivity, and then leaps recklessly from a helicopter, machine gun blazing, and lights up everyone he sees. Then he takes another pill to bring his mood back down to a manageable level, and off he and his pilot go to New York, following orders placed by a general but dictated by the man blackmailing that general—the Kingpin.

Bringing in someone like Nuke to handle the Kingpin's Daredevil problem is utter, literal overkill, and that suits Kingpin just fine.

THE MAN HE IS
LEARNING TO
FEAR.

MURDOCK.

Matt Murdock, oblivious to this new threat headed his way, is busy helping Karen Page wage a war of her own. We're reintroduced to the former couple through an overhead view of the Hell's Kitchen building in which they are currently staying, rendered in lovely, lived-in detail by Mazzucchelli.

Karen's eyes are shut tight, the tears streaming from them very different from the ones she shed at the end of the last chapter. Her withdrawal is eating her alive. But Matt is there, his eyes also closed, but a more serene look on his face. They can get through this.

As Matt holds the frail woman, her thoughts are presented in less chaotic fashion than that of her physical form. She reflects on Matt's response when she told him what she had done, how she brought all of this damage into his life. "Nothing," he told her, "I've lost **nothing**." Which is when she's made aware once again that she hasn't totally destroyed the core of what made Matt a hero. She might have given up his secret identity, but she never told them what she knew about his superhuman senses.

And more, she thinks—she never told them about the **man**.

As raw and exposed as the two characters appear in Mazzucchelli's title splash, the page awash in Max Scheele's pale color palette and plenty of negative space, Miller's words are tender. They're hopeful.

The printed version of Mazzucchelli's art for this page was corrected from what he originally drew, after then-editor-in-chief Jim Shooter asked to have her gaunt face softened a bit.

Unfortunately, the page as printed was also placed incorrectly so the artwork didn't run full bleed (the art extending off the page). Subsequent printings have run the page as it was originally intended.

In a wind-strewn park, Ben Urich meets with Foggy Nelson, as both sides compare notes about the Kingpin. Urich feels out Foggy for information about Matt as well as the Kingpin, but Foggy doesn't know why his blind partner would be involved with any gangster. Urich knows why, but he isn't telling.

The papers they're comparing get scattered in the wind, and while helping gather them, assorted photos that Nelson had tucked in among the paperwork reveal to Urich the photographic chops of Glorianna O'Breen. Glori, at a crossroads, has been out photographing the city's denizens. Urich wants to bring her into the *Bugle* for work.

But even as her employment status looks to be changing for the better, Foggy Nelson finally realizes that his own new employer might not be on the up-and-up.

Karen Page is sleeping, the worst of her addiction throes perhaps behind her. Or maybe her slumber seems more peaceful because she's fallen asleep cradling Matt Murdock's Daredevil costume, the other remnant from his former life. Matt's not ready to wear the suit again yet. Matt may never be ready to do so, even as he shaves off his new beard, but if it gives Karen comfort in this way, so be it.

STAN LEE presents

GOD AND COUNTRY

by FRANK MILLER and DAVID MAZZUCCHELLI

MAX SCHEELE
COLORS

JOE ROSEN
LETTERS

RALPH MACCHIO
EDITOR

JIM SHOOTER
EDITOR IN CHIEF

Mazzucchelli's rendering of this image of Karen asleep on a rickety twin bed echoes his visual approach to the previous images of a sleeping Matt Murdock. While her sleeping arrangements aren't anywhere near the level of Murdock's old brownstone—this one is all exposed plumbing and rough-hewn lumber under skylight glass—Karen now looks at peace in ways Matt never did in this series.

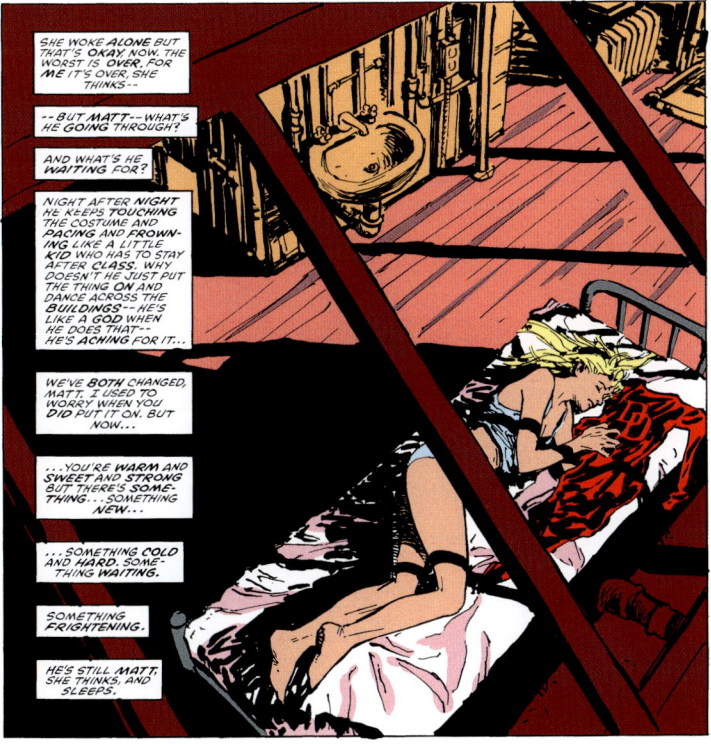

Ben Urich continues to investigate the Kingpin. He's been let into the nurse Lois' cell, with new *Daily Bugle* photog Glorianna O'Breen at his side, to get Lois' version of the events that led her to this prison cell. Only two of the cops turn out to be associates of the Kingpin, and they promptly murder Lois and Urich's bodyguard. They're about to do the same to Glori when something in Urich spurs him to action. He disarms one of the men and beats him to death with the man's own pistol. All the while Glorianna's camera keeps snapping photo after photo of the events.

The final image in the scene, again effectively presented from an overhead angle, is a silent one filled with dead bodies and with Urich, a pleading look in his eyes as he sits astride the man he just beat to death, looking at Glori.

> I AM, IN THE *STRICTEST* DEFINITION OF THE LAW, A *CRIMINAL*.

Ever the master manipulator when he can't simply resort to blackmail—as we've seen Kingpin embrace with the various cops, businesspeople, and military leaders in this story who have helped him execute his plans against Murdock—Wilson Fisk now turns his attention to Nuke. Kingpin lies to Nuke about the status of his son, discussing the enemies who brand him a criminal and who obviously hate this country. He also sows doubt that the media can be trusted, physically embraces the flag that was newly installed in his office to prove his patriotism, and generally manipulates the damaged, violence-prone Nuke into fighting Kingpin's battle for him. Nuke, his eyes bulging and neck straining in anger at what Kingpin tells him about his enemy, demands to know where this villain can be found.

"Hell's Kitchen," he replies.

In Hell's Kitchen, a still-recuperating Matt Murdock has taken a job as a fry cook in a diner. Which happens to be the place where Ben Urich and Glorianna O'Breen stop to grab a bite and discuss what they've been through.

It's also a diner that is right in the path of Nuke's helicopter, which arrives on the scene and swiftly drops down above the city street, allowing the heavily armed, heavily medicated soldier to leap out, guns once again a-blazing.

Nuke fires indiscriminately, destroying buildings and lives with reckless abandon. Matt's enhanced senses unfortunately make him aware of each painful loss around him.

The diner explodes. The building where Matt and Karen are living collapses in an explosive burst. War has come to Hell's Kitchen.

Murdock rushes to the carnage at his building. *Karen.*

She's somehow still alive amidst the building's rubble, and still cradling Matt's costume. Matt assures her she's safe now.

NEXT: **ARMAGEDDON**

For the past few issues, Matt Murdock has had nothing to do with his Daredevil alter ego. Even after fighting his way back to health and sanity, the form of protection he offered those around him came from Matt, operating from the shadows, not Daredevil. Daredevil was the cause of all that had gone wrong in his life of late—even beyond just the events of "Born Again." It felt as though Matt realized his return to a healthy place needed to come from within and first allow Matt Murdock to be born anew. Maybe there would never be a need for Daredevil again after all.

And then the Kingpin and Nuke served as a harsh reminder that Daredevil was still needed, necessary.

It's then that Matt Murdock comes to terms with his alter ego once again. It's then that he dons the outfit that he needs to help ensure that Karen Page and others don't fall under the sword the way others close to him have. It's in this moment, after all this time, that Matt Murdock stands as Daredevil once again.

Chapter Seven: "Armageddon"

The action on the cover of *Daredevil* #233, "Born Again's" concluding chapter, fairly explodes off the page. Battling characters—Daredevil, Nuke, and, curiously, a new player:

Captain America—overlap one another in front of an explosion which expels energy lines overlapping characters and logo alike. The title logo overlaps a corner box at last showing Daredevil in costume once again. The image is layer upon layer upon layer, the largest of which is the explosion of yellows and whites that further illuminate the primary colors of the combatants. The issue's title, "Armageddon," once again occupies the bottom quadrant of the cover. Only on the cover of chapter four, "Born Again," did the issue's title appear atop the cover images.

"This issue respectfully dedicated to **Jack Kirby**" reads the only caption on the issue's page-one splash image. Which seemed curious at the time, since Daredevil was one character that Jack Kirby rarely illustrated, and had no reported hand in his creation. But Jack *was* the artist/co-creator of Captain America, with writer Joe Simon.

The dedication was one of two discussion points that Macchio had with editor-in-chief Jim Shooter about this issue. Shooter maintained that it wasn't Marvel's practice to dedicate comics to anyone and asked that the dedication be removed, but he ultimately relented. As he did on a more pertinent story concern that we'll get to.

The splash page itself is a beautiful Mazzucchelli image of a rooftop water tower crumbling under a massive explosion vividly colored by Scheele, as Daredevil's much smaller form tries to survive that same blast.

The loss of that water tower is impactful as the action that opens the issue continues Nuke's fiery devastation of Hell's Kitchen. Daredevil, back in costumed action in ways he hadn't been since the story's first chapter six issues ago, evades Nuke's automatic gunfire on a rooftop bathed in seething yellows and greys, as the fire rages around him and the neighborhood of his birth.

Nuke takes the fight in close. Matt thinks he's up for the challenge, but finds that Nuke's body has been accentuated with non-human enhancements such as a version of the super-soldier serum that once gave Captain America his powers, indestructible plastics, and a steady diet of pain-deadening pills.

The fight is going poorly for everyone but Nuke and the Kingpin, who is watching the carnage without care for civilian deaths or that the chaos is upsetting the many people in thrall to the Kingpin who are also high-profile residents of the city. His vendetta against Murdock is all that matters.

Ben Urich and Glorianna O'Breen survived the diner's destruction and remain nearby, documenting the action. Until the action gets a bit too close and Glori is peppered with rapid fire from the low-flying helicopter.

Desperate, with no other options available, Matt uses the momentarily incapacitated Nuke's gun to destroy the helicopter, blowing up both the machine and its pilot.

Now, in the more modern era of comics and comics-related media, it's not uncommon for even the more righteous super heroes to kill.

But in 1986, and especially with a character who is fueled by his Catholic upbringing and his strong sense of morality, Daredevil was no killer. In "Born Again," both he and reporter Ben Urich were pushed far beyond their normal limits, and both resorted to lethal action against threats against them and their loved ones.

In Urich's case, he lost control; in the case of Daredevil blowing up both helicopter and pilot, his response was very controlled and deliberate—he saw no other way to stop the carnage that was taking the lives of so many people around him, and so he did what he felt he had to do to stop it. Neither man's actions had any lasting repercussions beyond this storyline, but it remains jarring to see the lengths they were forced to go to in order to stop the greater violence around them. Kingpin and Nuke brought war to Hell's Kitchen, and in war, there are casualties. As rendered by Mazzucchelli and Scheele, the explosive death of the helicopter pilot was visceral, a scene painted in extreme reds and yellows.

And then, out of nowhere, *they* appear. Some of New York's biggest and most powerful costumed super heroes: the Avengers Captain America, Thor, and Iron Man. These three Avengers bring with them a sudden rainstorm to quell the surrounding fires.

For the most part, Daredevil operates at a level below that of these more *super* heroes; while they regularly take on Earth-shattering threats, Daredevil is content to remain confined to his corner of the city, fighting lower-level villains and gangsters like Kingpin. These powerful Avengers appearing in this issue is jarring, especially in the way they arrive, with a desire not to understand or ease into the scene but rather to control it. Under Daredevil's watch, things spiraled out of control enough to finally catch their attention, and so they see themselves as necessary to save the day, no matter anyone's hurt feelings.

What's equally jarring and thrilling about this sequence is, much as the Avengers don't try to make nice with their fellow hero Daredevil, neither does he refer to them in his interior monologues as though he had any past association with them. The lack of character names also serves to separate them even further from Daredevil. They're super-powerful heroes who came down from on high, which is a perfect contrast to the street-level Daredevil. He doesn't refer to them by name because they're not part of his world, they're part of the world above.

Of course, those major Marvel heroes not being named in the comic also became the other point of concern that editor-in-chief Jim Shooter had with the issue.

As the initial action winds down thanks to the Avengers, Daredevil attempts to force a confession from Nuke that he was sent by the Kingpin, only to find himself on the receiving end of a threat from Iron Man to turn Nuke over to them on federal authority. Daredevil isn't crazy about this but he's even less wild about the power being aimed in his direction if he doesn't comply.

All of which has created quite a mess. For the Kingpin, and for the other syndicate leaders who confront him about the recklessness with which he has approached this vendetta (one of whom doesn't survive the experience).

But that's not a situation Matt Murdock has any time to worry about right now—he's too busy helping tend to survivors while staying out of Foggy and Glori's sightlines. He's not yet ready for that.

Many of the victims of Nuke's assault are laid out in the church where Murdock recuperated. Maggie the nun and other helpers tend to shooting victims like Glori, who needs care but is more concerned about her photos of the attack getting to the *Daily Bugle* as soon as Foggy can get them there. He's concerned about her new career choice. Miller creates enough of a crack in their relationship that the next series writer has an easy "out" if they choose not to keep the two of them together.

In this post-battle sequence, Mazzucchelli again displays real skill at portraying real-world settings and characters. More sparingly used are his abstract lines from the previous few issues; here, he's again portraying the world of Hell's Kitchen with all the detailed naturalism of the earlier "Born Again" issues. The overhead scene of all the victims lying on church pews, diffuse sunlight streaming pale warmth over all of them, is as gripping as effective as any super hero fight scene, if not more so. Mazzucchelli, already so good heading into the partnership with Miller, has proven throughout that he's a burgeoning comic-book superstar, although his muse would lead him away from Marvel and, soon after, away from DC and super hero comics in general, in service of an even more refined and unique artistic vision.

But first, there's a tale of "Born Again" to wrap up.

Matt Murdock's presence among the injured like Karen Page presents him as a man who seems once again at peace with the world and his place in it.

That is, until he senses the arrival of someone on the scene who has no business being there.

Matt hustles up to the rooftop to confront that person—Captain America.

Cap, ever the good soldier, wants to know what Matt Murdock knows about Nuke. Murdock tells him that Nuke is a physically enhanced terrorist, sent under the authority of Captain America's employers, the United States government. He wants to know why Captain America cares.

"He wears the flag," Cap replies. To which Matt, blind but also pointedly uncaring about the details involving the man who shot up Hell's Kitchen, replies, "I hadn't noticed."

He dives off the roof, leaving Cap standing alone and questioning the orders he was given.

Cap takes his quest for information further—he confronts the general who helped orchestrate the entire sordid Nuke affair, a man placed in that compromising position by the Kingpin. A man who tries to manipulate Cap by assuming he has sworn unwavering loyalty to god and country. Cap's not so easily coerced.

Working separately but with similar goals in mind, Captain America and Daredevil both dig deeper in their own unique ways. Cap infiltrates the deepest levels of the military base in search of information about Nuke—who, as it turns out, was indeed a recent recipient of a new version of the Super-Soldier Serum that gave Captain America his enhanced abilities during World War II.

Meanwhile, Matt Murdock again dons the red Daredevil suit: "[It] gives me a psychological advantage over criminals, Karen," he says to justify him dressing up once again. "Right, right," she replies. She knows who he is and why he is.

Matt wants to get his hands on some of the Kingpin's ill-gotten gains in order to help the residents of Hell's Kitchen rebuild their shattered lives. Kingpin, meanwhile, has also orchestrated making himself the recipient of an award that will legitimize him as a proper businessman among the New York business cognoscenti. Even amidst Ben Urich's revelatory articles about his wrongdoings, Kingpin is on the cusp of cementing his status as a source of true power in the city.

Captain America's situation is the more precarious of the two, since Nuke, located elsewhere in that same military base, reads one of Urich's particularly inflammatory articles about Nuke's boss and is driven into another blind rage. He busts out, fuels up on amphetamines, and plans to take the fight to Urich and the *Daily Bugle* offices.

Fortuitously, Captain America on the scene puts an end to these plans… but he is now beset by the military, who have been given a kill order of their own to ensure that the secrets Nuke carries are never made public.

Daredevil arrives just in time to save Cap's life, but Nuke takes some direct gunfire. Even with his body enhanced the way it is, he's not likely to make it through the day after suffering that level of abuse. Perhaps he will be silenced forever.

This harrowing sequence also has moments of levity, as the very blind Daredevil manages to get the grievously injured Nuke out of the base and then commandeers a taxi cab to transport Nuke away while there's still time. Matt promptly runs a red light that he cannot see, and then slams into another car. Enhanced senses minus eyesight aren't a whole lot of use when it comes to driving.

Those senses do make Daredevil aware that Nuke won't survive a trip to the hospital after all. So he changes course and heads toward Nuke's original destination—the *Daily Bugle*. He manages to make it inside the building, and our last look at Nuke and the costumed Daredevil in "Born Again" is a silent and chillingly effective one: one last overview view of the characters, this time showing Nuke's prone, seemingly dead body laid dripping wet and bloody on top of Ben Urich's desk. There's no chance of Nuke's story being buried now.

Things go poorly for the Kingpin. In one page, his carefully constructed life is undone nearly as completely as Matt Murdock's was: Some of his men confess to their part in the various messes his Murdock vendetta has left behind; others turn on him in different ways, leading to sub-committee investigations and seeing him stripped of awards. His status among the business community is legitimate no more, and pending litigation threatens to keep him tied up in court for years, his reputation irreparably damaged.

But again, in the Kingpin's eyes, none of that matters as much as what he did to Murdock. He, and we, know that he'll manage to rebuild his empire sooner or later. For now, as Kingpin reflects back on recent events, Mazzucchelli once again pulling in tight on Fisk's hate-filled eyes, the Kingpin reflecting not on what he has lost, but instead what he took from Murdock. Which isn't all that much, when it comes down to it. But, Kingpin thinks, he did take the law from him.

"Murdock," he thinks. And plans.

Comic-book adventures starring popular super hero characters rarely ever end. Not permanently, anyway. And no matter how this storyline resolves on its final page, the adventures of Matt Murdock as Daredevil are sure to continue on from here.

And yet.

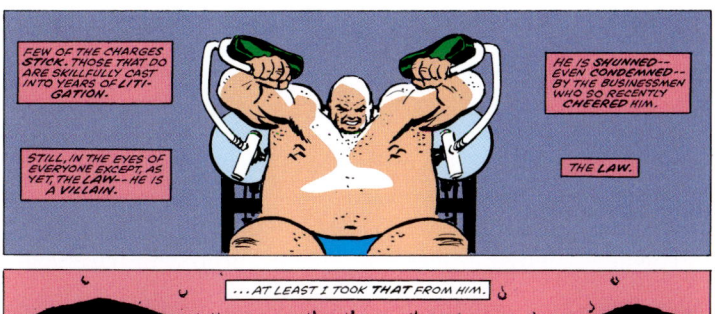

And yet the final image of this issue and this storyline is a final splash page showing not the costumed hero, determined to continue fighting the good fight, but instead Mazzucchelli leaving readers with a lasting image of a healthy Matt Murdock and Karen Page, dressed in plainclothes and walking the streets of Hell's Kitchen, signs of the city's reconstruction visible around them.

The page is signed by Mazzucchelli, which reads as his own "goodbye" to the character and the title (and soon, to Marvel Comics as well). Miller's captions on this page reflect a physically and mentally healthy Matt Murdock. It all reads like the final page of a final Daredevil story. At least, the perfect way this story resolved lands with a finality that makes the idea of more Daredevil stories feel unnecessary, or even grotesque, because the only way future stories in the world that is serialized comics work is if this moment of pure happiness *doesn't* last. It can't, and it surely won't (especially for Karen, come the time of the "Guardian Devil" storyline at the turn of the twenty-first century).

For now, though, Miller and Mazzucchelli, who have taken these characters and the title's readers on a truly harrowing journey from dark to light, deliver the perfect send-off:

> "My name is **Matt Murdock**.
>
> "I was **blinded by radiation**. My remaining **senses** function with superhuman **sharpness**.
>
> "I live in **Hell's Kitchen** and do my best to keep it **clean**.
>
> "That's **all** you need to know."

4

"A Man Without Hope is a Man Without Fear"

Crime lord Wilson Fisk, the Kingpin, was introduced to the Marvel Universe in the seminal 1967 issue #50 of *Amazing Spider-Man* (featuring the famous John Romita "I Quit" cover, a comic-book trope almost as common as the discovery of a character's identity.

As created by writer Stan Lee and artist John Romita, the Kingpin was originally portrayed as a massive, rotund but highly muscled figure with a smooth bald pate and distinctive suit. Though he was a prominent underworld figure even then, he also doted over his wife Vanessa, initially seen as an aged gangster's moll sporting long black hair with a shock of white running through it (at least, she appeared that way until Frank Miler was given permission to de-age her a bit in his first stint on *Daredevil*).

Wilson Fisk and Vanessa also had a son, Richard, with whom Fisk had a more precariously balanced relationship. While away at school abroad, Richard got wind of his father's career choice and he dealt with this in a completely normal way: by faking his own death and then assuming the guise of a mobster called the Schemer, who tried to cut into his father's turf. Eventually, the younger Fisk donned another secret identity as a dapper, leather-masked villain known as the Rose.

As mentioned, it was Frank Miller's handling of the Kingpin in his first *Daredevil* run that gave the character a new sense of menace and gravitas.

In Miller's third issue as *Daredevil* writer/artist, #170, he brought the character directly into Matt Murdock's path, which began their long, contentious relationship. In that issue, Kingpin's love for his wife Vanessa led to her being kidnapped and used to manipulate him into returning to the life of crime he'd chosen to give up. Seeking violent retribution against those who took her, Kingpin states his intentions clearly to his men about those who currently rule the New York underworld in his absence: "They have the men, the guns. But I am the Kingpin. I created the criminal empire that they presume to rule. I can bring it down, piece by piece. And if Vanessa is harmed, I will. The city will suffer a gang war bloodier than any it has ever seen. And my enemies will die… each and every one."

As this gang war spreads across the city, it results in Kingpin losing his wife (forever, he erroneously assumes), resulting in Fisk again assuming his former role of New York's Kingpin of Crime in order to make his enemies pay for what they did to Vanessa.

Which leads to direct conflict with Daredevil. Kingpin eventually hires an old Daredevil foe, Bullseye, as his chief assassin. Which is bad enough, but a year later, in Miller's run, Bullseye also kills another of Kingpin's assassins, the ninja Elektra… you know, Matt Murdock's former college flame? Suffice it to say that the enmity between Daredevil and Kingpin only grows along the way.

But then something odd happens. After Daredevil goes so far as to use the reveal that Vanessa survived to blackmail Fisk into calling off a promising, if corrupt, mayoral candidate in his employ, the two characters then reached a kind of equilibrium point, if not a full détente. Each began to see that the other could at times be useful. Both men, while driven by vastly different agendas and moralities, operate outside the law in their own ways. As with many gangsters and warlords, Kingpin does use some of his vast power to benefit (often in order to manipulate) people in the city. And Daredevil is occasionally driven to extra-legal means to accomplish his version of the greater good, too. Both men are at times given to using the other for the greater good (or bad).

As Kingpin put it to Daredevil in issue #190, "Consider also, Daredevil, that when you needed to **find** [a ninja hideout], you did not contact the **police**. You came to **me**.

"We **need** each other, Daredevil. We are **partners**, after a fashion.

"We are the **power** in this city."

That concluding scene in Miller's interpretation of their tenuous relationship makes the developments in "Born Again" all the more jarring. Surely no reader of comic books would take a villain like Kingpin at his word, but the ferocity he demonstrates in first destroying Matt Murdock's career and then his home life (and his home) is shocking. And even after accomplishing these things, the Kingpin can't let Murdock go. There's always been something about Daredevil's inherent goodness that Kingpin finds loathsome. Daredevil may manipulate a situation or break a law to get his way, but at his core, he and his intentions are good. To the Kingpin, a decent man needs to be torn down, broken, corrupted, and ultimately destroyed, lest that man rise again and show Kingpin that Daredevil's form of *good* can still win out over the Kingpin's more oppressive form of *bad*.

5

Broken Down and Rebuilt

Matt Murdock was in a downward emotional spiral long before the start of "Born Again."

Not so long after the murder of Elektra, his college girlfriend-turned-assassin, at the hands of his nemesis Bullseye, Murdock reunited with his former girlfriend, Heather Glenn. Only to then experience another tragic loss as Heather Glenn accepted Matt's desperate marriage proposal only to then take her own life.

Matt's relationship with heather was a complicated one. During their tumultuous time together, Heather discovered Matt Murdock's secret identity. (For all the *sturm und drang* in "Born Again" over the Kingpin's discovery of Matt's secret identity, it was never really the most closely guarded thing. Past villains such as the Death-Stalker [who met his final fate in Miller's first issue as the regular *Daredevil* artist] knew his secret, and elsewhere in Miller's first run, Bullseye even once puzzled out that he was Matt Murdock. He even revealed this to the Kingpin in issue #181, but Kingpin moved on from Bullseye, hiring Elektra as his assassin instead, and so he disregarded anything the unpredictable Bulleye had to tell him at the time.)

Heather, another of those close to Matt who discovered his secret, also blamed Daredevil for her father's death, further complicating their relationship. And after Elektra's murder, Matt Murdock tried to re-establish some kind of normalcy in his life by reuniting with Heather, but he was also dismissive of her attempts to assume control over her father's business empire. Their eventual engagement, only a few issues after Elektra's death, never seemed to bring comfort to either character, nor did it seem to be anything that Matt put much effort into. Heather was a life preserver for Murdock, who was already swimming in chaotic emotional seas following Elektra's fate. Heather felt that more and more, until finally she checked out completely with grim finality.

Too soon after Heather's death, Matt's professional life, and another attempt to stabilize his personal life through a relationship with Glorianna O'Breen, also hit some major stumbling blocks. There's perhaps another book to be written about Matt's codependence. Here, inevitably, due once again to the challenges of maintaining a secret identity, Murdock tried and failed to properly manage both sides of his life.

All of this together combined to create in Matt Murdock increased mental instability, and growing distrust even of his inner circle of friends and loved ones. Matt had always been tightly wound, experiencing lower lows than the generally upbeat people in his life like Karen and Foggy (in the old days, anyway). Matt is reeling from loss, unsure of himself and who to confide in. Which is where "Born Again" opens.

The crossroads where Matt finds himself at the start of the Miller and Mazzucchelli story grows progressively worse. Miller's portrayal of the character's mental decline is what gives "Born Again" such added emotional heft. Too often in comics of the past, a hero's secret identity was revealed only to have the status quo restored through magic, trickery, manipulation, or other such comic-booky contrivances, often before the end of a single issue.

Not so in "Born Again." In addition to Matt's breakdown, other characters also show evidence of mental stress, anxiety, and, in the case of the escaped lunatic who dons Daredevil's outfit in order to discredit him, complete psychosis. None of which feel glossed over or overly heightened to suit the dictates of the story. Rather, the way Miller employs mental illness seems to comply with legitimate medical reports and studies of mental disorders. To that end, this chapter looks at the various illnesses on display in the book, and the way their categorizations align with the characters' actions in the story.

When "Born Again" opens, the darkness that has always been a part of Matt Murdock's life threatens to consume all other sides. With no certainty over who he can trust, he decided he could trust no one. Never before had the character been portrayed with such deep and resonant personality disorders. It never felt contrived, and indeed developed naturally over years of anguish-inducing pain and loss that both Miller and writer Dennis O'Neil had the character experience in their prior time on the title.

Interestingly enough, even while working on "Born Again," Miller also explored the idea of another character suffering from schizophrenia in a *Daredevil* graphic novel released the next year, October 1986's *Daredevil: Love and War*, illustrated by Bill Sienkiewicz. In that story, the character so afflicted was the villain of the piece, not its protagonist. In *Daredevil: Born Again*, it's the heroic lead character of the title who has to contend with his slide deeper into various mental distress.

The delusions which Murdock experienced early on in "Born Again" were all points on a compass that pointed him in the direction of the one man who seemed responsible for all of it: the Kingpin. It was easy for Murdock to believe that forces were conspiring against him when, in fact, that was proven true soon enough.

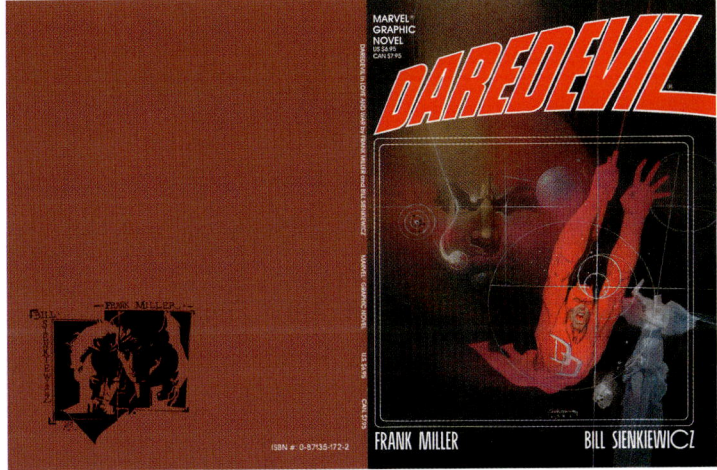

At first, the signs were mundane—his power was shut off; his bank accounts were frozen—but then a man he'd always known to be a good, honest cop had told damaging lies about him that helped ruin his professional life; when he called his friend Foggy's house, his girlfriend answered.

At that point, with his career in tatters, his house in pieces, and his finances locked away, the entire foundation of Matt Murdock's former life was destroyed. And with it, his ability to fend off the dark thoughts that always threatened to encroach on his life. As a result, Murdock's paranoia tipped over into psychosis, as he believed he was being conspired against, his every move sabotaged by another player in this harmful game.

Even more disturbing, as his difficult situation began to escalate, his delusions grew: He mis-heard voices on the phone and imagined friends, and even an automated time operator, were part of this perceived conspiracy. With no one to trust and everyone else's motives now suspect in his mind, Matt's extreme paranoia took root and grew throughout the first half of the story.

But anxiety and paranoia are only part of the symptoms that Miller brought to life in "Born Again." Others were on display as well, through Murdock's deeds as well as his words, and they were further compounded by his past experiences, too. At his lowest ebb after an adult life filled with battle, trauma, and loss, Matt Murdock was susceptible to other factors that helped contribute to the mental distress he experienced over the course of these seven chapters.

Matt Murdock had spent his life fighting for right, whether with his fists as the costumed Daredevil or in the courtroom as a lawyer. He was convinced of his own inherent goodness, and as the careful life he'd constructed crumbled away along with his secret identity, he experienced a kind of post-traumatic stress disorder, where the overwhelming trauma from so many external events made him feel even more disconnected from his life and his loved ones. With the safety of his established life and his network of friends gone, as well as the security he once knew, Matt's defenses against the complex interplay of psychological, emotional, and physical challenges that his dual life have created is stretched to the breaking point. His life has lost all control.

In such an emotionally weakened state, Murdock's best defense was the emotional disconnection he began to experience, as well as an inability—or even a desire—to regain control over a life that had lost all control. His once more measured approach has given way to fits of rage and despair.

Being Daredevil is, at the best of times, immensely physically taxing in addition to the emotional toll it takes to maintain a dual identity. In "Born Again," maintaining that identity and fighting crime became toil without end, especially once the Kingpin's machinations removed his relative safety and security. Murdock's fatigue became more than physical; it took a grave emotional toll on his mental well-being, too.

Surely all of these experiences, including the loss of multiple women with whom he had relationships, had also exacerbated his already refined sense of guilt. Murdock was raised a Catholic and, from his earliest days, he has had to grapple with both his waxing and waning faith as well as the guilt he feels in betraying his father's only wish for him: that he develop his brains rather than his brawn, which is something Matt's father, Jack Murdock, failed to accomplish as a low-level boxer in debt to the mob.

Murdock's personal and professional relationship with best friend and business partner Foggy Nelson was already fractured at the time his romantic relationship with Glorianna O'Breen likewise hit the skids—both casualties of his attempts to maintain his dual existence—so Murdock withdrew further, his emotional range vacillating between emotional stiffness and extreme irritability (that occasionally tipped over into rage). He was losing control and his emotional state suffered greatly. Which in turn led to additional lapses in judgment and helped exacerbate the unease he was already feeling.

These lapses were further evidenced by the clear, vivid hallucinations Murdock began to experience at the same time. He heard the voice of the motel proprietor as one of the Kingpin's stooges; worse, after he makes a phone call to an automated time operator, he experiences that robo-call as the voice of his friend Foggy Nelson, giving Murdock permission to kill the Kingpin. Conversely, he interprets the voices of other friends and confidants as being conspirators in on the plot to destroy his life.

Soon after, as Kingpin's man observes when Murdock boards the subway to follow through on "Foggy's" permission to kill the Kingpin, Murdock displays a marked decrease in interacting with his environment. As others near him on the subway get robbed at gunpoint, Murdock sits calmly, unreactive. He maintains a rigid, inappropriate, or bizarre posture… at least until a gun is pointed at his face. At which time, his well-honed instincts as a fighter and super hero take over. Of course, even this more normal (for him) response is taken too far, as Murdock beats the would-be thieves and a nearby policeman, too. He's at his lowest emotional ebb.

By pushing away his loved ones through his words and actions, Murdock's world further unraveled. His isolation from friends, employment, purpose, and even shelter all compounded to lead to the near-total breakdown he experienced. In a comic-book series where the hero usually wins out, it's especially hard to watch.

Since their inception, comic-book adventures involving super heroes with secret identities have touched on the identity crisis that such a split can cause in that character. Dual identities are challenging to navigate at the best of times, and in "Born Again," Matt Murdock is about as far away from good times as any comic-book character has ever been. The life he once knew is gone, so what is left?

For a while, only darkness.

Fortunately or not, since his early childhood, Matt Murdock has been no stranger to darkness—the loss of his eyesight and then, not long after, his only surviving parent (as far as he knew) forced him at an early age to navigate such emotional and physical minefields. Which is perhaps also the only thing that ultimately saved him from his fall in "Born Again."

Left with nothing but darkness, all other trappings of his life stripped away, Murdock is left only with his well-honed ability to fight; to never give in or give up. His father may not have been able to leave him with much but he did impart that. And it turned out to be the most valuable possession he has. "Never give up, never..." he thinks, even while in the throes of his breakdown, and while being pummeled by the Kingpin's fists, and it's this simple mantra that he clings to and manages to live up to throughout all of his travails.

All of which leads to a more complex portrayal of, and unraveling of, a super hero's psychological health than many comic books tend to offer. Even more than the physical trauma Matt suffers throughout this story, the dual toll his struggles take on both his body and his mind help highlight the extreme costs of maintaining a dual existence.

6

The Marketplace

Frank Miller's initial stint on *Daredevil* made the title a hit almost immediately. The comic, which was a middling comic for Marvel in the pre-Miller days, quickly rivaled the landmark *X-Men* series by Chris Claremont and John Byrne for top-seller status.

And history repeated itself when Miller returned to the series in 1985. When *Daredevil* #227 launched in October of that year, the series was still a solid seller and the character a fan-favorite, riding as it had on the coattails of Miller's original time on the book. The industry publication *Amazing Heroes* ranked it in the number four slot of its top ten titles of 1985, but its sales no longer crested the way they did in Miller's heyday.

Before his return, Marvel's annually published reporting of the US Postal Service Statement of Ownership, Management and Circulation showed that *Daredevil* sales in 1983–84 averaged 177,884 copies per issue.

After the launch of "Born Again," the title's sales climbed to an average of 189,959 copies per issue. Miller and Mazzucchelli's pairing on the title brought in more fans and plenty of acclaim from reviewers in the comics press, too. The Miller and Mazzucchelli run hit its peak with the concluding issue, *Daredevil* #233, which exceeded 208,000 copies sold, including newsstand sales, per internal Marvel tracking via John Jackson Miller's Comichron.

About "Born Again," *Amazing Heroes'* Reviews Editor R.A. Jones said in issue #86 (January 1986), "This tale of madness and murder was psychological drama of the highest order, tight as a violin strong." Further, Jones had similar praise for David Mazzucchelli's artwork, nothing that Mazzucchelli "has taken an art style similar to [classic *Daredevil* artist] Gene Colan (though clearer in focus) and developed it into a truly outstanding graphic form."

Jones also wrote, "*Daredevil* is now at a fever pitch of intensity that matches that of [DC Comics's acclaimed horror title] *Swamp Thing*—with a level of violence and bloodshed that far exceeds it… making *Daredevil* a book one feels an urgency about reading. And we'd best enjoy it while we can—according to the grapevine, Miller will not be with Marvel for long. While he is, this book should be savored."

The Comics Journal reviewed *Daredevil* #227—the first chapter of "Born Again"—in issue #105 (February 1986). The *Journal's* attitude toward super hero comics was typically somewhat dismissive, as their focus tended to be aimed at independent (non-super hero) comics and graphic novels. But they too found much to love in the first issue of Miller and Mazzucchelli's run, stating, "Boy, is Frank Miller good at this stuff," and "I should mention that artist David Mazzucchelli holds up his end quite well with nothing fancier than a flair for characterization." The review concluded with, "It's Miller's show and welcome return it is."

The creators got off to a critically well-received start, although *The Comics Journal* did revert a bit more to type in its following issue, #106 (March 1986), when reviewer Heidi McDonald delivered a panning of the issue's story and art. However, even she reached the conclusion that "Miller has a story to tell, a mood to impart, and characters to put through the wringer. In this hyperbolic underworld, he's created a unique fictional universe. And that's why I'm reading Daredevil again, just to find out how the story [that Miller began on his initial run on the title] ends."

In *Amazing Heroes* #88, only two issues after the magazine's report heralding Miller's presumably long-term return to the title, they reported that, instead, *Daredevil* #233 would be Mazzucchelli's final issue of the series and the conclusion of his time at Marvel. The publication announced that Miller was leaving as a result of Mazzucchelli's departure but would remain on the title for two additional issues, to be drawn by Miller's old studio-mate, and fellow writer/artist auteur, Walter Simonson.

However, as it turned out, Miller's final issue on the series matched Mazzucchelli's: issue #233. His planned two-parter, entitled "The Devil's Own," never got beyond the first script. According to Miller's script, one of the developments in this "Born Again" follow-up is the specific revelation that the nun, Maggie, was referred to directly as Matt Murdock's mother, a fact heavily alluded to but not outright confirmed in "Born Again."

When asked about the gestation of this two-part tale and why it never came to pass, in 1997, Walter Simonson told the website manwithoutfear.com, "To the best of my knowledge, Frank never scripted part two. I never did pencil part one. And the reason was that *DD* was getting a new regular writer at the time after several fill-ins. The new writer wanted his first issue to come out at the beginning of the summer (the good sales period back then) so our two-parter was put on hold for a few months. And if there's no deadline, the work never gets done—that's an old freelance rule. The gist of it is that by the time Marvel was interested in having us work on the story, Frank was off doing *Dark Knight Returns* and I was off doing *X-Factor*. So it never happened. Too bad—it was a cool story."

In the mid-1980s, comics' most prestigious award was the Jack Kirby Awards, which were awarded from 1985 to 1987. At that time, the awards split into two separate awards: the Eisner Awards, named after graphic-novel pioneer Will Eisner, and the Harvey Kurtzman Awards. In 1986, Miller and Mazzucchelli's work on the title was awarded with four nominations and two wins: *Daredevil* #227 won the Kirby Award for Best Single Issue, and Miller and Mazzucchelli also won the award for Best Writer/Artist (Single or Team) for their work on the title. The same team would be nominated again the following year for their work on DC Comics' *Batman: Year One*. Despite starting in late 1985, *Daredevil: Born Again* is one of the foremost reasons why comics historian Peter Sanderson of *Sequart* referred to 1986 as "The Year That Changed Comics."

With the benefit of hindsight and owing to a number of acclaimed and impactful releases issued within the same calendar year, 1986 is now considered one of the most important years in comics history. One of the key reasons for this is that a number of the more popular and still-discussed releases had a darker tone than comic fans were used to. Taken as a whole, these graphic novels contributed to an overall shift toward a darker, more adult tone across many comic series that followed. "Born Again" was released ahead of other notably dark and more serious super hero titles from 1986: *Watchmen*, Miller's *Batman: The Dark Knight Returns,* and Miller and Mazzucchelli's *Batman: Year One,* as well as Marvel's *X-Men* event series that crossed into a number of other titles as well, *Mutant Massacre.*

7

Born Again and Again

As I've been exploring throughout this book, stories involving the revelation of a character's secret identity have been a tried-and-true way to create peril for a character. And in nearly all such stories over the decades, those revelations—indeed, you could say the same about most changes to a character in comics—have not been lasting, nor had far-reaching consequences. Typically, any such revelation has been undone quickly, and the status quo resumes, thanks to using a doppelganger to gaslight the person who discovered the secret, amnesia, mind-control, a deal with the devil, or maybe even spinning the earth in the opposite direction of its axis—all have been employed to mind-wipe the civilian who discovered this big secret.

But "Born Again" was not so easily undone. The unraveling of the character's identity and his personal life wasn't reset at the end of the story. The Kingpin disappeared in disgrace but the knowledge of who Daredevil really is hasn't been wiped from his memory. Matt Murdock's disbarment hasn't been undone.

As happens in comics, future *Daredevil* writers did move past the storyline, lessening its initial impact and moving Matt Murdock's story in other directions. But its repercussions were felt in other writers' follow-up stories.

Series editor Macchio stated that at first, it was hard to settle on a proper follow-up to "Born Again":

What's interesting is that I'd talked to several writers about following up on Frank's work, but many of them were unsure because Frank's run had made such a huge impact. Some people saw it as a challenge and were excited to take it on, while others felt like, "I don't know how I could top that." It became a bit difficult.

I remember that at one point, Steve Englehart was going to write the series, but there were some creative differences about the direction the book should take, so he ended up not coming on. But here's the interesting thing: I also had a conversation with writer Ann Nocenti [a Marvel editor and writer who did enjoy had a long, acclaimed run on the series, working primarily alongside the wonderful art team of penciler John Romita Jr. and inker Al Williamson].

Ann [...] wasn't intimidated by Frank Miller having been on the book before her—she was more than willing to take it on. I was impressed by the few issues she'd done, and she had a solid grasp of the character.

Nocenti developed stories that allowed Matt Murdock to pivot back toward a legal career while also remaining a champion of the oppressed in more direct ways than in his "Nelson & Murdock" days; later, writer Kevin Smith picked up on storylines and characters from "Born Again" in his Marvel Knights launch (with tragic consequences). Brian Michael Bendis' subsequent long-running storyline, beginning with "Underboss," involved the even-more-widespread dissemination of Daredevil's secret identity, a clear follow-up the developments in "Born Again." That story then begat Ed Brubaker's run as writer, which built even more on the revelation of Murdock's identity and his imprisonment as a result of that news; and then Mark Waid's time on the title led to a more carefree and swashbuckling version of the character who nevertheless still had to contend with the world knowing Matt Murdock was Daredevil.

Eventually the revelation of Murdock's identity was erased, only to have it revealed again... and then undone again. (So it goes in the soap-operatic world of serialized comics.) But the initial shadow cast by "Born Again" remains long, which speaks to not only the strength of the story but also to its timelessness. A character's secret identity being revealed and then his life destroyed by gangsters and the regular people in his thrall could have been told in the 1940s or in 2020.

It wasn't the first to do so but "Born Again" not only laid a new blueprint for future comic writers to follow in terms of the exploration of identity, but it also helped show that in the discussion of what it takes to truly be a hero and fight on against all odds; there are few who would ever do so more effectively than Miller and Mazzucchelli.

8

Conclusions, Impact, and Lasting Resonance

Following the finale of "Born Again," which ended with a happy and healthy Matt Murdock and Karen Page reborn as a couple, the task facing subsequent creative teams was considerable: To pick up directly from where "Born Again" left off? To once again contrive events to drive a wedge between Murdock and Page, so newly reunited? To manipulate the story to allow another super villain to tear down the world that Murdock had so tenuously managed to rebuild? Or to head in another direction entirely?

For the first issue in the post-Miller/Mazzucchelli world, at least, Marvel chose the latter option. *Daredevil* #234, no longer the planned Miller/Simonson follow-up story, instead told a standalone story that didn't connect directly to "Born Again" but rather offered a story that hearkened back to the character's more trouble-free era.

Subsequent writers, most notably Ann Nocenti, then followed the path first trod by "Born Again" in terms of maintaining "Born Again's" status quo (Karen Page, the Hell's Kitchen setting, Murdock's employment as a short-order cook rather than a lawyer) for a time. Nocenti brought an outsider's perspective to the series, less beholden with what came before and instead focusing on stories that demonstrated her more humanist approach to storytelling. As good and stylistically different from Miller's as her stories were, she also had the good fortune of being paired with artist John Romita Jr. for the majority of her run. Nocenti and Romita Jr.'s time on the series was marked by a unique degree of empathy, one that felt both different from Miller and Mazzucchelli but also a natural evolution of the series' characters. The Matt Murdock from "Born Again" was a character forever (for now) changed but also one whose life pivoted enough to allow the series to continue without re-treading familiar ground.

As stated at the outset, the idea of super hero creative teams exploring the revelation of a hero's secret identity and all the resultant fallout from such a development is fertile, if commonly trod, ground. More often than not, eventually that secret will again be treated as such, and those in possession of such knowledge will end up mind-wiped, killed, or removed from current continuity, or the secret otherwise hidden away once again. And with good reason: Super hero comics are largely intended to tell ongoing stories of the never-ending battle between good and evil, and the more lasting developments that are layered onto any such character will eventually so greatly limit the storytelling options that it becomes unfair to both the current readers and current creators. It's neither a good nor bad thing that ongoing tales of super heroes necessitate the occasional reset; audiences age or move on, and new audiences deserve to experience stories that thrill them in the way that "Born Again" thrilled readers at the time and in the decades hence.

And for all the creators who follow it and decide to explore the ins and outs of a character's identities, it continues to serve as a guiding light to help illuminate future stories, as its beacon continues to shine brightly for so many who have experienced it.

As this book has explored, there are a number of salient reasons why the issues that make up the *Daredevil: Born Again* storyline continue to resonate and reverberate across the decades. There are storyline reasons; lessons to be drawn from its sales; strong characterizations and memorable writing; gorgeous art and colors; and other deeper, meaningful explorations of loss, heroics, mental health, and other unique aspects of the story and art on display throughout. But ultimately what it comes down to is:, Did and do readers find the story compelling enough to revisit it over and over, despite the passing of decades and the hundreds of issues of *Daredevil* that have come since its release? The answer to that has come in the form of the book's constant presence on bookshelves. "Born Again" has been released in deluxe oversize editions, digest-sized books, massive tomes that display replicas of David Mazzucchelli's original art boards, new softcover editions, large hardcover editions, and digital collections. All of which serve to remind people of the comic's strength from the outset.

Daredevil the character and the comic have continued to reach new heights over the decades since "Born Again" was released, and the character has thrived in other forms of media beyond just comics as well. Once Frank Miller's initial efforts elevated the character to revered status, it's a designation that hasn't slipped since. All long-running comic series feature high points and points less high, but the bar originally set by Miller, Janson, and Mazzucchelli remains an aspirational high-water mark for subsequent creators to aspire to. Of course, all opinions of their work, directions chosen, and stories told will vary from reader to reader, but the fact that *Daredevil* still features so many echoes of these original stories serves as ongoing tribute to what these creators brought into the world.

Similarly, Frank Miller and David Mazzucchelli have continued to develop and grow in interesting and surprising directions, and their evolution as artists and storytellers likewise continues to inspire new generations of creators and readers.

Daredevil #227 through #233 was a unique pairing of two master creators, and its influence continues to be felt today. It holds up on repeated readings, and if this book accomplishes anything else, it's to inspire you to read it once again and experience its wonders anew.

The storyline's name is *Daredevil: Born Again*.

It was created, written, and drawn by Frank Miller and David Mazzucchelli.

It's waiting to be revisited again and again.

It will provide a rewarding reading experience each time you do so.

That's **all** you need to know.

ACKNOWLEDGMENTS, CREDITS

The death of Elektra changed my life.

In my earliest days as a comic reader, I was a Fantastic Four kid. And then along came Spider-Man. And the Hulk and the Avengers and on down the line. Daredevil operated beneath my notice for a time. He just didn't strike me as cool enough to justify me plunking down additional quarters every month for his comic.

Until my comic-shop provider talked me into checking out that landmark issue of Frank Miller's first go-round on the title, *Daredevil* #181. I didn't know who Elektra was, and I suppose there was something odd about being so moved by the violent death of the character in that issue since this was my first exposure to her (and to the storytelling prowess of Frank Miller). But her death had real resonance. I felt it. And I wanted more of that feeling (not death, I mean, but comics that made me even as a preteen yet to experience much real life really *feel something*).

Daredevil became my jam. **Frank Miller** became my jam.

So among the many people who deserve thanks for this book, foremost is Frank, along with longtime *Daredevil* inker and often colorist too, Klaus Janson, whose finishes delivered a perfect blend of darkness and light, along with the watchful stewards like Dennis O'Neil and Ralph Macchio. To them, and to those who followed Miller's run and continued to hold my attention in different but equally captivating ways, this book is respectfully dedicated. As it is to David Mazzucchelli, whose art was a joy to experience and whose artistic development was even more thrilling to watch.

As I learned by digging into the Miller-drawn back issues, there was another player deserving of attention, too. *Daredevil*'s turn from a somewhat ordinary super hero title into what it would become under Miller started with writer Roger McKenzie, who established the blueprint that Frank built upon. Roger is perennially unsung in comparison to higher-profile writers who followed, but his time on the title should be lauded by others as it is by me. Here's to you as well, Roger.

Daredevil may be blind but my affection for the character and his world isn't; that is due solely to the work that all of the above creators, and so many before them all the way back to his creators Stan Lee and Wally Wood, have brought to the title. This book only exists thanks to them and so, you know, thanks to them.

On a more personal level, I fed my Miller *Daredevil*

addiction thanks to the efforts of my mom, Patricia, who drove me every week to the comic shop—which was nearly an hour away—so that I could pick up every issue the day it was released. Which finally started my own *Daredevil* collection after years of having to borrow my brother Ken's copies.

Finally, ample thanks are owed to everyone whose help on this book made it all possible and, in each case, helped make for a better end result: Marvel's Sven Larsen and Ralph Macchio, Ted Adams, John Jackson Miller, Annie Nocenti, Silenn Thomas, and the Bloomsbury team.

The best part about making comics is the collaborative aspect, and making books without pictures is no different.

The other best parts are the people who sell and read comics, and both those parts of the comic-book machine are invaluable, and deeply appreciated. Thank you for the support you've given me and my books over the years, and even more, thank you for caring about this medium as much as I do.

ILLUSTRATIONS

ADDITIONAL
BIBLIOGRAPHY

De Jong, Bruno Savill. "The Man Without Fear...By the Year: Daredevil 1986, 'the Most Important Year in Comics'—Comics Bookcase." *Comics Bookcase*, September 9, 2021. https://www.comicsbookcase. com/features-archive/daredevil-comics-1986.

Sanderson, Peter. "1986, the Year That Changed Comics: Introduction." Sequart Organization, n.d. http://sequart.org/magazine/15257/1986-the-year-that-changed-comics-introduction-part-1/#google_vignette.

ABOUT THE AUTHOR

Chris Ryall, a luminary in the comic-book industry, boasts a prolific career as a writer, editor, publisher, and historian.

Ryall is the co-founder and CCO/publisher of Syzygy Publishing and the former Chief Creative Officer/Editor-in-Chief at IDW Publishing.

As a writer, he has co-created *Dreamweaver, Zombies vs Robots (ZvR), Groom Lake, Onyx, The Hollows, The Colonized*, and *Dread the Halls. ZvR* was purchased by Sony Pictures for feature development. He has also written graphic novels based on *Shaun of the Dead, The Transformers, Rom Spaceknight, Weekly World News, Kiss*, and *Mars Attacks*, and has collaborated on graphic novel projects with Stephen King (*Road Rage*), Clive Barker (*The Great and Secret Show*), Harlan Ellison (*Phoenix Without Ashes*), and Francis Ford Coppola (*Megalopolis*).

He is the co-author of *Comic Books 101* (IMPACT Books, 2009) and *The Mighty Marvel Calendar Book: A Visual History* (Abrams ComicArts, 2024), and editor/writer of Simon & Schuster/Gallery13's line of deluxe Marvel Fireside reissues:

Origins of Marvel Comics, Son of Origins, and *Bring on the Bad Guys.* Ryall was an Executive Producer on Netflix's three-season *Locke & Key,* EP on BBC Studios' in-development *Eve Stranger,* and is the co-creator/co-writer of *The Bullpen,* a scripted series in development at Paramount. His upcoming releases include *Marvel House of Horror* (Dark Horse), *Francis Ford Coppola's Megalopolis: The Director's Cut* graphic novel (Abrams ComicArts), and *Marvel Corner Box Art: A Visual History* (Abrams ComicArts).

MARVEL AGE OF COMICS

Explore the series!

www.bloomsbury.com/marvel-books

The Mighty Avengers vs. the 1970s
by Paul Cornell

The Avengers was **the** comic book of the 1970s. From Civil Rights to Women's Lib, battles for the soul of America became battles between super heroes.

Doctor Strange: A Decade of Dark Magic
by Stuart Moore

The story of one of Marvel's most bizarre, otherworldly heroes, beginning with his creation at the hands of Stan Lee and artist/plotter Steve Ditko, and discussed against the backdrop of one of the most turbulent decades in American history.

Spider-Man: Miles Morales
by Ytasha L. Womack

A look at the hugely successful reimagining of one of the most popular super hero characters of all time.